AESTHETIC STUDIES

Architecture and Poetry

AESTHETIC

ARCHITECTURE &

Katharine Gilbert

AMS PRESS
NEW YORK

STUDIES

POETRY

FOREWORD

This LITTLE BOOK must be shelved under *philosophy*. No other kind of writing was possible to me. But of this kind it is again a kind: not the result of manipulating abstract relations nor of fixating pure essences, but of natural wonder about things going on around us in the arts. Architecture and poetry were the two arts that drew me most, not because the other arts were not wonderful and perplexing, but because words said about these two by specialists and practitioners happened to meet my meditations halfway and to fertilize them. For example, a little while ago I read that a room was the essential architectural expression and then I learned that the up-to-date and informed spoke not of rooms at all but of areas and tensions. Where then has the *room* gone? Or if not the room as such then the "room of her own"? And when is a building a crystal and when a climate?

As for poetry, this art obviously did not wait till today to touch philosophy, though their present encounter is in a new mode and raises fresh questions. Yeats for instance, one of us, made ancient Plato the archinquisitor of contemporary values. But in his own time Plato wrote and judged poetry. The permanent interdependence of the two—philosophy and poetry—is best conveyed for me by the recounting of an incident that occurred in Athens in 1936. On his last night in the ancient city an English schoolmaster asked a boy of twelve if he would like to be a mountain goat with him and climb the Acropolis in the darkness. As the man and the child pushed their way up the ascent, the first said to the second: "What are you going to be when you grow up?" "A poet," replied the child with simple promptness. "Ah, that is fine," said the older one, "but in that case you will need to know a great deal of philosophy." This claim, though obscure, is to my mind valid; and its converse equally so.

I wish to express my thanks to the editors who kindly allowed republication of material from their journals.

Katharine Gilbert

CONTENTS

SEVEN SENSES

OF

A ROOM

"SEVEN SENSES OF A ROOM"
WAS DELIVERED AS THE PRESIDENTIAL
ADDRESS AT THE MEETING OF
THE AMERICAN SOCIETY FOR AESTHETICS
AT HARVARD UNIVERSITY
SEPTEMBER 4, 1948

In 1933 Laurence Binyon, delivering the Charles Eliot Norton Lectures at Harvard University, reported the following experience:

Some years ago I chanced to visit the house of a collector in London, and without preparation, after admiring the pictures, stepped from the modern house into a room designed and built by Inigo Jones, which the owner had bought entire and had had set up afresh as an adjunct to his house. It was not a very large room, but it seemed spacious, partly because of its loftiness, partly because it was empty of furniture, though panelled in wood throughout. It is strange how suddenly one can change one's mental climate. I seemed to have stepped straight into the seventeenth century; into England as it was when a plain majesty of style, the style of the Authorized Version of the Bible, came naturally to speech and pen, when also the glories of the Italian Renaissance were beginning to impress their forms upon art and architecture, as they had already coloured with flame the poetry and drama of England. It was like, I thought, inhabiting for a moment the mind of Milton. . . . Those simple yet stately proportions, that austerity of ornament, that disdain of the trivial which yet communicates no sense of emptiness but rather of latent richness—these belonged to Milton's native air, to the time in which he lived. . . .

. . . that stately room of Inigo Jones's . . . seems a symbol, if only we complete it with a garden, enclosed, well-ordered, with turf soft to the feet, trees to shade the sun, flowers to delight with scent and colour—a piece of nature trimmed and subdued to human pleasure. The bare and lofty room is a fit place for the mind at home "in the spacious circuits of her musing," as Milton puts it; the ordered garden a place of solace and refreshment. Here is nature mastered and put to service; here is the mind within its fortress.[1]

In this report of an old pleasure, a sensitive scholar—former keeper of prints and drawings in the British Museum—records a wide variety of aesthetic impressions. The very casualness of the account symbolizes its freedom from bias. What Mr. Binyon says is not the necessary premise of a wished conclusion. He speaks neither as Freudian nor Gestaltist; neither as idealist nor materialist; neither as art-historian nor analyst of structure or function; neither as a literary nor a visual semanticist. Quite definitely he does not speak as a professional aesthetician. Indeed he shies away from the name and concept of aesthetics. At the end of the series of lectures from which our quotation is taken, he contrasts the common man's freedom in the enjoyment of art with the business of aestheticians. Aestheticians frame definitions of art, he says. Their knowledge is knowledge about. Ordinary mortals—and he includes himself among these—enter in, and take their fill and roving range of pleasures.

Now surely Mr. Binyon is wrong about aesthetics—at least about the aesthetics celebrated here and now. No competent aesthetician ever wished permanently to isolate the defining of art from the enjoyment of its values, not even such aestheticians as some teasing boys in the profession like to call by uncomplimentary names and suspend off in a basket in the clouds. As proof of Mr. Binyon's error about aesthetics I intend to use his excursion on the Inigo Jones room as a clue to one kind of aesthetic analysis. Why? Because a room is exceptionally rich in aesthetic dimensions. An aesthetic analysis bent on inclusiveness finds a peculiarly favorable field in the room. It goes without saying that connoisseurship here will make much of the aspects of architectural order: symmetry, proportion, balance, scale. Mr. Binyon notes the "simple yet stately proportions," the spacious effect due to loftiness and emptiness, and the closed and connected pattern of an imagined garden-extension. Of course any work of art would show order. An architectural example, however, involves mathematics (that source and arbiter of meticulous patterning) more persistently than other kinds; and its kinship to engineering is closer. But granted that species of order are not peculiar to the room, its literal enveloping power is. Many things that are not one's self can be very intimate to the self, but they stop short of a room's power of assimilation. The poet Hopkins once said that a man "hoods or hats himself with the shelter of a roof, a penthouse, or a copse of trees." He thus suggests how close to the body and soul of man something spatially external—like a tree or roof—can seem. But a man standing in a room is in the heart of a distinguishable spatial thing—swims in it like a fish in a wave. The French art-historian Foçillon[2] and the French poet, Valéry, point to this marvel. Valéry in his dialogue *Eupalinos* says:

A painting covers a part of a wall; a statue fills a part of

5

the visible field. But an interior forms a kind of complete volume within which we live. We exist; we move about; we live inside a thing that a man has made. One might say that we breathe in, there, somebody's will and preferences. We are held and mastered in the proportions he has chosen.[3]

This being within a room and feeling oneself part of it Mr. Binyon also notes, as he runs over the facets of his experience. He has been absorbed into a new climate, he says. He breathes a different air. He feels himself inside a mind. The qualities of his surroundings communicate to him a sense of "latent richness."

Besides the shapely proportions of the room and its total absorbing quality, Mr. Binyon notes other aspects: the room is for him a fortress, a symbol, and an analogue.

My purpose in this brief essay is to elaborate the suggestions in the Binyon text toward a tentative list of various aesthetic senses of a room. The seven modes I name are of course abstractions. In the actual imaginations of persons (witness Mr. Binyon's), in the concrete occasions, as in the attributes of styles there is overlapping of mode, and variety of motivation. And as there is plurality in the modes of apprehending aesthetic forms, so there is plurality in the methods of discovering modes. No priority is claimed for the method used here. Stimulated by the efforts of others, particularly Herbert Read's,[4] I simply undertook a survey of my own. I became convinced that the "room" is a superior testing ground, and that literary comment is unusually revealing.

I shall first briefly list my seven modes. After that I shall attempt to characterize and relate them and speculate on the reasons why people make such emphases. The tentative list follows:

1. *The cell or fortress mode.* Delight in solidity and finality, and in the presence of obvious shape and protecting bounds.

2. *The porch or "organic" mode.* Delight in immediate connection with nature; with sun, air, the landscape, and whole stretch of space.

3. *The impalpable essence mode.* Fancy for a "personalized" interior; its impregnation with a mood-color, such as mauve; or with a permeating, arbitrarily chosen quality, as of a scent, or archaic aura.

4. *The harmony mode.* Use of a set of proportions or color scheme intended to produce an effect conceived of as "musical."

5. *The surprise, humor, or tilt mode.* Conceits find expression in rooms as in poems.

6. *The reminder and symbol mode.* The dressing of walls with images more or less conventionalized. Infiltration of "literary" meaning into visual form.

7. *The functional mode.* Control of form by prospective use, with climax in the devising of an appropriate place for a celebration.

The first two modes, the fortress sense and the porch sense, stand in such natural tension that it is practically impossible to treat them out of relation to each other. Mr. Binyon in the passage that is our original text holds them in counterpoise, letting them symbolize the Occident and Orient respectively; and everyone knows that Frank Lloyd Wright sets his tree-like architectural living-space in sharp opposition to the "prettified cavern of our present domestic architecture."[5] "The box idea," he says, "is the reverse of free."[6]

But a room designed by Inigo Jones is not merely unfree—a prison to escape from, as Mr. Wright would try to convince us. The fortress form has characterized a long-enduring style and satisfies certain permanent demands of the human spirit. Though the values of continuity with nature and the far vista—typical of the wise and gentle Chinese temper—are more congenial to Mr. Binyon, he himself appreciates the values in the Palladian architectural habit. It may strike him as harder and more arrogant than the Eastern way, but it springs equally from human need and philosophy. He ends the passage we cited, you will recall, by an interpretation of the human meaning behind the seventeenth-century room: "Here is nature mastered and put to service, here is the mind within its fortress," "a piece of nature trimmed and subdued to human pleasure." This is the theme Mr. Binyon repeats in the various books in which he compares the spirits of Eastern and Western art. "There is nothing which divides the East and the West so fundamentally," he writes in his *Landscape in English Art and Poetry,* "as . . . the difference in the conception of man's true place in the Universe, and his relation to the world about him. . . ." "Is man the centre and the lord of all things? Or is he but one among a million existences which make up the living universe?"[7] Binyon answers again and again that Western man glories in his dominance, in this erection of great walls that exclude all lesser or alien things; in that passionate assertion of the ego against the world, which has inspired the vast monuments built by great conquerors, in the imposition of order and definition on all the wild and uncontrolled variety of nature.

According to the methodological or scientific background of the period, the imagination that requires a fortress, and boasts of its finality, may assimilate its maker to divinity or to the beaver. God was often fancied as an Architect by the men of the Middle Ages and Renaissance, and a person rejoicing in the cosmos of a domed chapel or a Palladian palace hall could perform the reverse act, and fancy the architect god-like. For a spectator standing in the midst of a well-planned inclosure seems to be surrounded by the lining of a world created by man, though at human scale. At times he seems to boast: "This shell which I inhabit came into being through my power and at my order. Through reason, I can reckon. By reckoning I measure out the place I will inhabit. By mathematics I construct orders, relations, and patterns, and round out a thing. This self-contained entity harmonizes part with part through my tools of ratio and proportion. My reason makes everything agree and consent with everything else, so that the whole is final—perfect." This subconscious boast is charged with the same emotion as is a law of fate or a self-evident truth, except that in this case the human being is the proud Author of the fate and truth.

However it was more the 'fashion centuries ago to confer divinity on a maker of fortress structures than now. The overtone of satisfaction in the walled inclosure is traced nowadays to the vestiges of animal instinct. The bird builds its nest, the beaver its dam, the bee stores its treasure in a cell, and so can man make his secure lodging —only better. The quality of this biological root is not single: it includes protection against wind, weather, and living foes; the curling up in comfortable warmth in one's own proper element; the feelings of constructive ability, security, peace, mildness, exclusion of one's not-kind. Hobbes in the *Leviathan* made our habit of locking the door proof of his basic philosophy of the instinctive war of all men against all. So the lock on the door, if one stands on the right side of it, and of the whole protective equipment of stout walls, may become the sign of the human haven; a bounded volume organized into safety in the midst of surrounding chaos. Reference to this room-haven is everywhere in literature. "The refuge of safety, of softness, of vantage . . . enveloped in an amplitude of sure protection," writes Santayana.[8] "The healing of the blessed and uninvaded workroom," writes Henry James.[9] The castle-sense of aristocratic guarded aloofness and the peasant's sense of fireside coziness are variants of the same feeling. To sum it all up and hint at its latest scientific overtone, I may quote a casual confession from a friend's recent letter: "I'm afraid I have a kind of back-to-the-womb pleasure when I find myself comfortably at home in a well-furnished 14th or 13th century interior."

The second room-sense in our list must be understood, we have said, as the complement of the first. If Mr. Binyon delighted to find himself entertained and invested by the perfect, austere, and proportioned spirit of Inigo Jones, he delighted even more to find himself in the presence of the tombs of the Ming dynasty. These lie in the valleys among the hills near Peking. The approach to them, Mr. Binyon tells us, is marked by an arch or gateway. The tomb itself is no thing made by man's power; it is rather the landscape itself, selected, determined, and animated for its eternal function. ". . . the silent amphitheatre of hills gradually becomes . . . part of an august design; . . . the hills themselves in their solitude and grandeur . . . have been persuaded to enfold this valley of the dead and to become their 'everlasting mansion.' By submission rather than compulsion the unknown architect has conceived a sepulchre more enduring and sublime than any man has ever built."[10]

No one has conveyed more richly and delicately than Mr. Binyon the overtones of the porch or organic mode of apprehending a room, the pleasure in immediate connection with nature, with sun, air, animals, plants, water, hills, and the whole infinitely receding landscape. This sensibility, he says, "has discovered a harmony between its own life and the life of nature; there is a flowing out and a flowing in."[11]

But Mr. Binyon provides rather the most general postulates of a room in the mode, than a characterization of the room itself. Mr. Wright, touched by the Oriental spirit, but with his own genius for architectural invention, is more direct. The room, he says, is the essential architectural expression. But the room, logically and sensibly conceived, grows outward and becomes the house, which now rejects its old box-next-to-box nature; and, having become the house, which is flexibly organized into functional units by screens, it joins the world of nature. It plants itself in the earth, "grips it," and follows the horizontal earth line; it opens itself to light and air through the continuous casement. Though keeping to his good carnal sense of steel and concrete, Mr. Wright yet goes all the way to the literal interweaving of human fiction and the untouched earth. "My sense of wall was not a side of a box," he writes; ". . . [the wall] was increasingly to bring the outside world into the house, and let the inside of the house go outside. In this sense I was working toward the elimination of the wall as a wall to reach the function of a screen, as a means of opening up space." And he "fought for outswinging windows because the casement window associates the house with the out of doors."[12] His lyrics in praise of the synthesizing power of the "super-material" glass[13] are echoed and outdistanced by what Gyorgy Kepes says: Synthetic materials such as glass and plastics integrate spatial vistas and make inside and outside flow into each other. Reflections and mirroring, transparent and translucent materials can focus divergent spatial senses into one inclusive grasp.[14]

In characterizing Modes *1* and *2* I spoke of their natural polarity, but avoided jargon captions for antitheses such as extravert and introvert, classic and romantic. A more tenuous polarity may help to establish the meaning of Modes *3* and *4*. They are both methods of seizing and shaping the environment, commonly referred to as "aesthetic." The third mode washes or perfumes a room with a single or easily manufactured sensuous quality. The infusion is vague but gives the place a recognizable feeling. The socially ambitious housewife with her fluent decorator achieves a period room, a "blue room," or a "personalized room." Mode *4,* while concerned with effect, composes color or dimensions and arrangements with more knowledge and finesse. The one is a gross procurer of provocative interior flavor; the other, an architectural musician.

In recalling the kind of awareness he enjoyed of his childhood home Sir Osbert Sitwell writes: "I loved the impalpable essence—what later one learns to call the 'atmosphere'—of the house, a strange prevalence . . . pervading the mind like a scent faintly detected, the smell of wood smoke, for example, that seems to color a whole room with its fragrance though a year has passed."[15] So a child or childish older person swallows, as it were, a place whole.

It tastes bitter or sweet, or feels rabbity or silky, or floats in shadows or gleams sunny-warm and golden bright. The more elementary senses seem to determine its nature for a little-disciplined receptivity.

But such a provocative and haunting flavor as lingers in a child's consciousness, as if of the smell of cheese and beer, can be deliberately induced by the decorator. Sir Osbert remarks that about 1900 with the rebuffs to English prestige in the Boer War the confidence of the people suddenly wilted. And then it was that the interior decorator arrived to lift moods by judicious use of color. The fashionable mauve was liberally applied: ceiling, wallpaper, draperies, even women's clothing were given the fashionable tint. It is difficult to understand how the omnipresent mauve would lift the depressed feelings of the dwellers in the house, unless, as Sir Osbert suggests, the color really smelt like a lighter, brighter form of royal purple![16]

Today the decorator goes at the production of mood in a room with somewhat more science but with disconcerting assurance and a broad brush. Read these directions for room treatment: "Appreciate the energy in color. Imagination becomes reality through the use of color dynamics. The entrance to your home should be as friendly as a handclasp . . . as heartwarming as a smile . . . color dynamics works . . . to modernize the old-fashioned 'Welcome' on the door-mat . . . A dining room that sparkles with fresh, glowing color—a meal appetizingly served—and your reputation as a hostess is assured. Quiet reposeful colors help banish nervous tension. Grayed blue for relaxation and a sunny tint of yellow for a mild life—this combination logically induces a feeling of comfort and well-being."[17]

The feeling of comfort and well-being induced by the "impalpable essence" of mauve or rose, Colonial or Second Empire, stands in contrast with the satisfaction induced by a taut harmony of aesthetic relations. Room-sense *4* requires good proportions and subtle tonality of the wood paneling in the room designed by Inigo Jones. It would be difficult to praise a room in the Palladian tradition without using terms denoting harmonic ratio. In his recent long and learned analysis of the principles of Palladian architecture, Dr. Rudolf Wittkower[18] has not only set before us the balance and symmetry of Palladian buildings and rooms, but has followed in detail the roots of the Palladian set of values: the Pythagorean discovery of the mathematical basis of harmony in music, and of order and correspondence in the universe. After tracing the habit of thought which issued in Palladio's establishment of absolute ideal proportions and symmetries in architecture, Dr. Wittkower also notes its collapse beginning with Perrault's declaration in 1683 that proportions please for no other reason than that we are used to them. Perrault also declared the parallelism between beautiful visual proportions and pleasing musical harmonies merely conventional.

The question for us becomes: Is custom all? Is there no discoverable rationale behind the immediate demand for a pure shape or a special order of tone and form? If there is no classic form compulsory on men of good taste at all times and places, are there not, even so, deep-seated human ways that explain formal choices? Fashion, custom, accident do not seem adequate to explain Berenson's identification of the meeting of four arches under a dome as "the perfection of space,"[19] or the matching of tones in a Vermeer-like interior, or the lacework of Whistler's field of vision.

The answer that I have been able to work out is this: Nature presents infinite possibilities of form and arrangement but no decisions as to good form. (At least this seems to be true at first thought.) The range of light and dark is given, but not a scale with distinct steps: the spectrum dictates no adjustment of its hues to man's delight. This apparent absence of value gives support to the long-echoing modern disclaimer of the theory of art as imitation of nature—even of beautiful nature, because there is no beautiful nature—an alphabet, perhaps, which man articulates; or a keyboard on which he plays; but no model.

But one realizes after a while that nature, so conceived, is nature defined artificially by the very human being who is trying not to foist his own values on her. Nature lives and moves, as well as exists and contains, and she exhibits preferred ways of motion and life. And in the end man, the child of nature, finds his own preferred ways of working continuations of nature's habits.

Paradoxically, nature gives man the clue to her own subordination. His need for strength leads to intuitions of lines for strength in hillslopes and falling water; of direct lines in crystal formation; of stable and resistant pyramids in massed rock or well-based beast. Having the capacity for self-consciousness, man caps his intuitions with a sense of values and builds his art on nature's intimations. But man goes further. He can extract these same lines of economy and force, and the arch of ultimate dominion from nature's bodies, and completely harmonious tonality from a kindly luminous day. Such completeness Van Gogh condenses and symbolizes by his program for his bedroom: "walls pale lilac, floor a faded broken red, chairs and bed chrome yellow, pillows and sheets a very pale lemony green, quilt blood red, washstand orange, basin blue, window green," which add up, in their polyvalent complementariness, to "a feeling of perfect rest."[20] The completeness of the bounding arch of heaven Brunelleschi can essentialize into the modest dome, visible all at a glance, of the Pazzi chapel. The incidence of curve on curve in animals' necks and teeth and tails, or of mountain crest against mountain crest, devisers of ornament can make intimate in a brooch or border. Indeed, the reminiscences of nature's suggestions become almost lost in man's free handling. Thus a set of proportions or a color scheme gets to seem an abstract harmony. As a little musical figure floating apart in the realm of sound multiplies the possibilities inherent in its contour and rhythm and so generates a fugue; so a little figure of color, or ratio of height of door to height of wall, seems to proliferate by itself in the independent "life of forms."

But these apparent abstract harmonies are simply far wanderers from home. What seems autonomous matching and sparring has some kind of human meaning and scale in the end. I am making no reference to empathy. The man with a room-sense requiring harmony is one thing, and the room that gives it to him is another. But when the demand is happily met it is as if the two were partners in a dance. This sort of perceiver tends to swing his intuitive comparisons, and the terms judged fall into his rhythms. For we all carry around inside us flexible individual meters: a personal light-scale and metabolism rate; breathing balance, an attention gauge, idea span, and pace norm. And when all our interior pattern vibrates in time with the pattern of our ambient, a delicious comfort courses along the nerves. So it was the sense of beauty came to Santayana's hero Oliver Alden when, standing for the first time on the swaying poop of a schooner moving steadily out to sea, he felt how "everything trembled and everything held."

There is not much evidence of the fifth room-sense in our practical and efficiency-loving culture. We have light verse, but not much humorous room planning, except where fancy sometimes releases sea horses or curly tailed piglets on bathroom walls to match the morning tub's exuberance and whistling. Or in a cut-corner attic bedroom the black and yellow wallpaper may show a whimsical grouping of Gibson girls, gramophones, and pickaninnies flanked by words and music from "Sweet Adeline," "Swanee River," and "The Sidewalks of New York." Santayana has dubbed rococo architecture "comic,"[21] and examples of its fantastic forms are described in Sir Osbert Sitwell's autobiography; for example, a ballroom whose ceiling was ornamented with feathers, and whose walls were covered with Louis de Vos tapestries. The room, says Sir Osbert, was filled with a strange haunting element in which floated pearls and elephants, garden vistas and trophies, like salamanders in fire.[22] Another fantastic room was his grandmother's sitting room. Its ceiling, he says, was lofty and painted mauve, and the walls were lined with Indian hangings where scarlet monkeys disported themselves among the spatulate leaves of palm trees. "Against them, carved Burmese figures rippled their sweet hips of sandal and cedar wood, and on the tables and the piano . . . Indian draperies swept down to the ground, winking their thousand wicked eyes of looking glass. On the tables . . . stood orchids, stove plants with foliage that might have set the pattern for all the flags of the South American

republics, and cactuses . . . squat, fleshy creations with
patches of iridescent color and with thick, pulpy, serrated
leaves, that gave one the idea that an octopus must have
been changed into a plant, as Daphne into her tree."[23]

The sixth room-sense is "literary" and requires symbols.
You will recall that Laurence Binyon felt the presence of
the mind of Milton in the Inigo Jones room. But the suggestion of Milton could have been reinforced and made
explicit by carved or painted themes taken from *L'Allegro,
Il Penseroso,* or *Comus.* The room would have lost its reserve and simplicity, but might have acquired another rich
dimension of meaning. The shapes that constitute literary
tradition, that fill out a classical scholar's mythology, would
have become ever-ready companions for the occupant.
Murals and portraits and tapestries may give body and
brilliance to a man's justified joy in his great family heri-
tage or his literate humanism. Why should it be architecturally valid to integrate a room with the circumam-
bient rocks and leaves and sunshine as Frank Lloyd Wright
would have us do, and not architecturally valid to integrate a room with the climate of classical culture? Surely
a whole man may covet a whole environment. It is ad-
mitted that the principles of sound building should not
be contradicted by meaningless excrescence. But it is not
meaningless to house with a man food for his memory
and imagination. In 1562 Taddeo Zucchero received directions for such catering in the treatment of the walls and
ceilings of a Cardinal's bedroom. The great man was to
lie down to rest and to wake once more within a protecting shell lined from end to end with literary allusion.
Homer, Ovid, and Pausanias were to lull him and divert
him. The program of the whole was to be the varied il-

lumination, occupations, and associations of Night. In the eastern end of the ceiling, Dawn as Aurora in billowing slashed garments, white, golden, and red, was to ride her golden car, strewing roses. Near her, carefully disposed, were to be her bent old husband Títhonus and her fair lover Cephalus. The symbolic figure of Vigilance, a crowing cock on her head, was to seem striding into the room through the eastern window.

At the western end of the room was to be the counterpart of all this, the figure of Night with her twin children Sleep and Death, mounted in her bronze chariot. Her companions were to be Atlas and Ocean. The symbolic form of Repose was to offset Vigilance. Repose would be poppy crowned, and near her feet a brooding hen. The Cardinal should see Morpheus making masks and dream children with wings and crooked feet. Figures of major importance were assigned to positions in the great ceiling-oval and the crescents and pendentives. But around the room was to run a frieze, full of comic little creatures, placed under their proper quarter of the night; under Dawn, Petrarch's little Spinner ungirdled and barefoot, lighting her fire; hunters rousing to the horn; muleteers on the move; smiths turning to the forge and—students to their books. Opposite these, people of the shadows, spies and adulterers, with their fit animals: bats, owls, porcupines and hedgehogs.[24]

All the interiors that answer to this room-sense bring in absent meaning to enrich present circumstance. It can be such old fable and symbolism as we have cited, or it can be emblems of social significance such as the panels picturing the sower, ploughman, potato diggers, harvesters, and shepherds that Van Gogh set in the walls of a goldsmith's dining room.[25] Again it can be such images of rest and innocence as William Morris prescribed for wallpaper: the "many-flowered summer meadows of Picardy"; "a close vine-trellis that keeps out the sun by the Nile side"; or "the swallows sweeping above the garden boughs toward the house-eaves where their nestlings are."[26]

There is no need to linger long over Room-sense 7, because functional architecture and therefore functional interiors are today every intelligent person's choice. "Architects, critics, and historians," says Mr. James Fitch in his recently published book *American Building*, "have too long carried on their discussion of aesthetics in terms of literature, not life."[27] Literature without life is a ghost. American Gothic laboratories without proper sinks and Palladian auditoriums with poor acoustics are paper entities and not proper human environments. The imagination has learned to ask what shapes and lights and relations make steps fewer, seeing easier, cleanliness possible, and all the work of man less burdensome. But if a literary aesthetic not solidly based on functional requirements is ghostly, a functional aesthetic unmindful of the possible spread of human interests is thin. For what after all is function? Activity directed to an end; and of ends man has an uncounted number. It is a mistake to associate "functional building" with the more obvious physical usages of man, basic as these are. A man may need a spacious room not only to breathe in, but to think in. Any want that genuinely stems from within is a "function" whether it is a temperamental order for gay and fantastic decoration, or for a library full of emblem books. In his 1918 essay on "A Possible Domestic Architecture" Roger Fry tells amusingly how he flouted the snobs and built a house which was merely the solution of the problem of his personal needs and habits. In that sense his house was functional. But his needs and habits extended beyond the requirement of light, air, security, financial availability, and the like. Among his "functions" was a scholar's predilection for the baroque palaces of Italy. He hated, he said, pretty, low-ceilinged Elizabethan rooms. So he gave himself a living room-dining hall in the grand baroque manner.[28] And who is to say he did not need it?

At the crown of man's needs are those for festival and ritual. Though in its purging onset Room-sense 7 is prone to stress health, economy, and efficiency in the obvious work of man, in its imaginative extension it includes worship and private and public rejoicing. Unity Temple was designed around its function, as have been the little, simple, straw huts emulative of Zen monasteries where the Japanese tea ceremonies took place. However, my guess is that thorough semantic and axiological studies of the architectural concept of function might prove enlightening. I am curious as to whether "function's" intention could stretch enough to include such values as those of Ruskin's "Lamp of Sacrifice."

NOTES

1. *The Spirit of Man in Asian Art* (Cambridge, Mass., 1935), pp. 9-10, 14-15.

2. Henri Foçillon, *The Life of Forms in Art* (New Haven, 1942), p. 24.

3. Paul Valéry, *Oeuvres* (Paris, 1931), Vol. A, p. 108.

4. *Education through Art* (London, 1943), pp. 138 ff.

5. *An Autobiography* (London, 1933), p. 353.

6. *Ibid.,* p. 300.

7. *Landscape in English Art and Poetry* (London, 1931), p. 5.

8. *The Last Puritan* (New York, 1936), p. 104.

Katharine Gilbert

9. *Notebooks* (New York, 1947), p. 111.

10. *Spirit of Man in Asian Art*, p. 14.

11. *Ibid.*, p. 15.

12. Wright, *op. cit.*, pp. 139-41.

13. *Ibid.*, p. 353.

14. *The Language of Vision* (Chicago, 1944), p. 79.

15. *Left Hand, Right Hand* (Boston, 1945), p. 135.

16. *Ibid.*, p. 261.

17. *Color Dynamics*, Pittsburgh Plate Glass Company, Department of Color and Design.

18. "Principles of Palladio's Architecture," *Journal of the Warburg and Courtauld Institutes*, VII (1944), 102-22 and VIII (1945), 68-106.

19. Bernhard Berenson, "A Word for Renaissance Churches," in *The Study and Criticism of Italian Art* (2d ser.; London, 1902), p. 68.

20. Van Gogh to Paul Gauguin, Arles, mid-October, 1888, in *Vincent Van Gogh: Letters to Emile Bernard* (New York, 1938), p. 104.

21. "Soliloquies in England," in *Works* (New York, 1937), IX, 74-75.

22. *Left Hand, Right Hand*, pp. 21-22.

23. *The Scarlet Tree* (Boston, 1946), pp. 127-28.

24. Annibal Caro: Letter to Taddeo Zucchero, *In Scelta di Lettere familiari del Commendatore Annibal Caro* (Milan, 1825), pp. 383 ff.

25. Van Gogh to Rappard, Nuenen, 1884, in *Letters to an Artist: from Vincent Van Gogh to Anton Ridder Van Rappard* (New York, 1936), pp. 170-71.

26. "Some Hints on Pattern Designing," *Collected Works* (London, 1910-15), XXII, 178.

27. *American Building* (Boston, 1948), p. 348.

28. *Vision and Design* (New York, 1924), p. 276.

CLEAN AND ORGANIC:
A STUDY
IN ARCHITECTURAL
SEMANTICS

A CURIOUS READER of the architectural literature of the last few years is struck by the recurrence of certain terms of praise applied to the new forms, for example, the word "clean." "A good word in architecture is clean."[1] Frank Lloyd Wright said this many years ago, and a reader sensitive to words will have noticed how frequently it is his ultimate sign of approval. For instance: "We may now live in prismatic buildings, clean, beautiful and new";[2] "straight lines . . . severely clean and delicate";[3] ". . . the clean, significant lines of sculptural contours."[4] And with machines and Shinto in mind he expands into: "Today it seems to me we hear this cry 'Be clean' from the depths of our own need. . . . Clean lines . . . clean surfaces . . . clean purposes. As swift as you like, but clean as the flight of an arrow."[5] In his *Autobiography*, as if hailing a glad day, he writes: "A sense of cleanliness directly related to living in the sunlight is coming."[6] Whatever his divergence from Wright otherwise, Le Corbusier also admires the clean. He testifies that it was the effect of the Acropolis upon him that made him a

rebel, the Acropolis with its "clear, clean, intense, economical, violent Parthenon."[7] Frederick Etchells, intro-
ducing Le Corbusier's *Towards a New Architecture,* speaks
of a house "hard and clean," with "fittings as coldly efficient
as those of a ship's cabin."[8] J. M. Richards has spoken of
"the triumphs of clean engineering"[9] and "the clean and
efficient" new style.[10] Prizes have recently been awarded
for designs for churches because they were "cleanly simple
and structurally straightforward."[11] Elizabeth Mock, ending
her essay *Built in U.S.A., 1932-1944* with appreciation of
the unique beauty possible in a bridge—the "spare and
muscular beauty" achievable there—comes to a period with
the phrase "the clean economy of the essential form."[12]

The frequency of this one "good word" is striking.
But others are common, for example, "logical," "economical," "constructive." Indeed, any word-sensitive reader
could verify the pervasive presence of the following ten
terms as carrying an assumption of positive value in contemporary architectural design: modern, clean, logical,
economical, basic, social, honest, organic, constructive, vital.

For observers of the ways of words these terms do not
remain in isolation, but dispose themselves in families of
terms, and mate with synonyms more or less exact. The
groups of terms having thus massed themselves generate
families of counterterms. One may envisage an architec-
tural-verbal situation with dynamic interrelations approxi-
mating this pattern: (1) A positive group of near-syno-
nyms: *clean,* pure, sharp, trim, hard, bright, tight, stripped,
stark, antiseptic, crystalline, uncluttered, naked, crisp,
sheer. (2) A sympathetic family of moral terms, cousins to
the first set, immediately recognizable both as of frequent
occurrence and of cognate intention: *honest,* candid, frank,

straightforward, virile, uncompromising, integral, restrained, ascetic, just, chaste, mature, orderly, dignified, right, courageous. (3) Another sympathetic group connoting analytical reduction: *logical,* scientific, rational, true, inevitable, basic, diagrammatic, valid, simple, essential, geometric. (4) A group of terms used for denigration and representing an architectural state of affairs uncongenial to the first, and by implication to the second and third: *ideal,* unreal, romantic, mixed, soft, murky, cluttered, untidy, misty, sentimental, emotional, traditional, subjective.

Though we have here to do with words and not with designs themselves, there can be no doubt that the architects who use the words intend them to apply to real architectural designs, for description and/or appraisal. The words do not compose a "literary" or "subjective" characterization of architectural facts, but are clearly taken to refer to properties that inhere in those facts. Semanticists approaching this double situation of words and shapes would agree that the words are intended to describe and to evaluate architectural facts. They would assume that a verbal design parallel to the visual design was being constructed. Such analysts would also be interested, however, in tracing the terms reflectively to their various contexts and in checking the values associated by the authors with the terms. It would not be strange if they disclosed ambiguities in the employment of identical signs, and tensions buried in apparent verbal agreements, so that the two designs might not fit together after all.

If this occurred, it would seem that suggestions of more than verbal interest might come out of the examination of language habits and preferences in the architectural field. Words, floating like veils over a philosophy of design, may cover up shifts in thinking and attachments to surprising values.

This can be shown in the case of our word "clean." A study of passages, illustrations, and references in which "clean" occurs gradually reveals at least four distinguishable directions of meaning of this favorite adjective. As associated with the triumphs of engineering, and its general economy and efficiency, "clean" architecture would simply signify building involving the minimum expenditure of energy and materials for the end desired. This is, of course, the basic virtue usually attached to "functional" architecture. But when functional architecture becomes self-consciously clean, it assumes a strong negative tone. Its first value involves expulsion: ejecting the irrelevant. All architectural elements are then termed irrelevant that have no basis in actual human need but are lifted out of a bygone culture for sentiment or ornament's sake, through literary allusion, secondary meaning, or inertia; offering what once was fitting form for an epoch's habits after the habits are dead. "This clearing away of the historic debris, this stripping to the skin, was the first essential mark of the new architecture."[13] Architecture that is "pure," then, in deed and intention cuts away the fatty excrescences of the traditional styles, the classical orders, cornices, and embellishments. From inner equipment disappear old carved furniture and heirloom silver and china. The purists of architectural language throw out the moldy rhetoric of Roman banks and Gothic churches. Nuances of color containing the impurities of gray reflect for them a feeble and lingering fancy for dimly remembered shadows and compare poorly with clean heraldic colors.

First of all, then, "clean" as an honorific term in architectural writing means relevance, and it becomes synonymous with "logical." A specific, practical purpose confronts the designer and his business is to build solely for that end. Here the value involved is concrete, practical, and verifiable. All the group of kindred terms that expand the idea of good logic belong with "clean" *(1)*, and dirt, as in the proverb, means something out of place. Close calculation, clear statement of what is wanted, and computation controlled by the limited, tangible, conscious goal sum up the intention.

The second association leaves metaphors for literal significance. It is a direct carry-over from hygiene, antisepsis, good housekeeping. Here may be noticed the conspicuous interest in sun and air, washing machines, bathrooms and kitchen equipment. It is no accident that Dean Hudnut, recounting in a charming fable the conquest of modern design over antiquarianism, points his moral with a washing machine. "The clean round washing-machine" with its "white and restful serenity" drove out, in his parable, attachment to highboys, mirrors, and glass chandeliers.[14] The same overtones of "the surgery and enameled bath" are acknowledged by Kenneth Clark, but from the opposition. "Art," he asserts, "must be slightly septic." He allows that modern functionalism has perhaps been a health-giving interval in the history of European building, as it has applied the cure of starvation and the cold pack.[15] In general, the wholesome character of sun and air is a common theme for the new architect. We have already noted Wright's remark: "A sense of cleanliness directly related to living in the sunlight is coming." Siegfried Giedion takes the evolution of the bath as one of the significant aspects of the command taken by the machine;[16]

and James Fitch gives a section to "When the Bathroom Comes of Age," in his recent *American Building*.[17] Le Corbusier calls good planning "healthy."[18] Associated with the overtone of health and sanitation in the term "clean" are allusions to the fit form and function of the athlete. The clean line of modern engineering is, we are told, like the economical cut and curve of a diver's leap.[19] Again, pure building would "show the naked wall in all its sleek beauty,"[20] and once more, a modern bridge is "spare and muscular."[21]

"Clean" may also mean for our writers the clean soul as well as the bathed, sunned, and taut body, and this is the third variant. The group of terms denoting moral character, beginning with "honest," has been given above. An example of this sense occurs in the boast that functional architecture is "virginal of lies." What is meant here by lies? "The hollow sham of axial symmetry";[22] "the multitude of dishonesties—the cornices and the columns, the fake palaces and fortresses . . . the dishonest use of the symbolic function. . . ."[23] More or less consciously, but at any rate commonly, architectural writers fold moral values in with engineering efficiency and sun baths: chastity, integrity, continence, directness. The expansion of meaning from pure and wholesome in the physical sense to pure and wholesome in the moral sense is natural. It may even be inevitable, for our hygiene stands to us, of course, for a kind of morality. But the semanticist is aware, even so, of a change in tone at this point from description to emotive metaphor. Just how appropriate the attachment to architectural design of terms primarily applicable to human character and motive may be is not to be too hastily judged. It is probably only those influenced by contemporary depth psychology and its symbolisms who would not cry "metonymy" and "question-begging" when moral values are allowed to ride in on material fact and shaped space as real aspects of an architectural situation. Certainly both the large class of architectural theorists and of semanticists who are sympathetic to logical positivism would label as nonsense such metaphorical language in architectural description. For how can you verify the virginity of a wall or the sincerity of a stone cylinder? If words referring to moral character in modern construction are not nonsense, they are at least rhetoric requiring scrutiny.

The fourth meaning of "clean" is an intensification of the first sense so high in degree that the whole conception appears to split and shows not only a new but ultimately contrasting meaning. Now "clean" architecture, we know, always involves stripping and purging. But the cleansing process may be directed against irrelevancies in a specific culture, region, individual plan of life, or building requirement, as in Meaning *1*, or it may imply pursuit of purification for its own sake and abstraction carried to the limit. There is a temperament that never rests until it comes to what it takes for ultimate, absolute, or supreme. Both mathematical logician and mystic seek the basic and the simple in this unqualified way, and a strain in recent architectural thinking moves toward the same limit.

The best example of architectural thinking in search of the absolute is the Russian theorizing that followed the Revolution as described by El. Lissitzky.[24] He begins his account by contrasting the new way of building in Western countries with the new way in Russia. The new way in the West, he says, was largely the result of mechanical invention. While new materials and techniques altered for Europe and America the scale and design of building, the alteration was in general external compared to what went on in Russia. In Russia the social and political revolution of October, 1917, signified an absolute beginning— a new page in human history. The new building in Russia has to be understood in terms of the demands and ideals of a new world, and not of new implementation.[25] The Soviet regime, Lissitzky continues, wished *"nicht nur weiter verbessern, ausbauen, sondern ganz neu umbauen, nicht nur konstruieren sondern rekonstruieren."*[26] The utterness of change, the cleanness of the slate, he makes vivid by saying that the architects had as it were to strip off their own skins and grow new.[27] The very conditions out of which the new building could proceed had to be created, without precedent and without a co-operating industry. It was in experimental laboratories, speculation, and imagination, that the conception of the new assembly places, offices, and housing came to birth.

While largely sealed off from the rest of the world, the new Russian architecture did feel the influence, Lissitzky says, of the Russian Suprematist movement in painting. Painting because of the flexibility of its materials and immunity from court control had gone forward. As the word "supreme" suggests, it had approached that state of absoluteness which for social reasons was bound to characterize the new building. Malewitsch, the leader of the group, pushed his analysis of the elements of painting to *Urelemente*, "primitive terms."[28] In form the ultimate is the straight line; in color, white on white. Supreme paintings built with these simples, and their world, presented a geometrical order, a *"Gegenstandslose Welt."* Malewitsch's own description of his pursuit of pure essence resembles a mystic's story. He went into the desert, he said, to find pure feeling's form.[29]

The crystalline metric invented by Malewitsch, colorless and mathematical, is architectonic, and automatically becomes the transfer station for architecture proper. Now construction thus committed to the bare essence of abstract mathematical forms and necessary relations sloughs off not only dead styles and unmeaning ornament but approaches the limit of excluding the rich variety of cumulative human experience. At this extreme it yields pure prisms and lonely cubes. A philosophy of nihilism is not far away.[30] We might call such thinking the fallacy of placeless abstractness—a fallacy more prevalent now than Whitehead's "misplaced concreteness."

In noticing the variants of the conception of "clean," "the good word in architecture," we have moved from its most concrete to its most abstract intention. "Clean" can be roughly synonymous with "thought through," in which case "clean" becomes only another word for "functional," "logical," or "efficient" with pleasant overtones of health and sparkle. It is not then used to implement a metaphysic or radicalism. But it can also signify an intense pursuit of pure form as such. Then it connotes an otherworldly mathematical ultimate. The extreme of this abstract tendency we illustrated from Russian Constructivism and Suprematism, where the ideal in art breaks from the control of the particular concrete occasion and any common circumstance.

Pursuing our semantic analysis, we may take a second term, "organic," also a favorite in recent architectural writing. Again it happens that we may gradually discern several directions taken by a single sign. For instance "organic" may mean like a crystal. The ideal of Russian Constructivism, says Lissitzky, was *"eine Welt kristallinischer Organik."*[31] Organized in the sense of the crystal apparently connotes an articulation of elements, tight, transparent, and spare; for whenever the word "crystalline" occurs in recent discussion, it implies austerity such as was our equivalent of the fourth sense of "clean." The crystalline is the strictly geometric, says Malewitsch;[32] and Moholy-Nagy identifies the essence of an organic form with the crystallization of its function.[33] Readers of Herbert Read's *The Green Child* will recall that near the end rock crystal is made both the embodiment of perfect order and absolute beauty and also the symbol of immortality "when the body, no longer recognizably human, but rather a pillar of salt, took on the mathematical precision and perfect structure of crystal."[34]

But "organic" form in architecture is oftener contrasted with rock structure than assimilated to it. It is so contrasted and diagrammed by Lennart Holm in his analysis of contemporary tendencies in Sweden.[35] There the crystalline principle is treated as mechanical, while the true "organic" is set over against it as individual and personal. But it is Wright, himself, who has fixed the association of "organic" architecture with the growth of trees, the life principle in seeds, and nature springing from the soil. Not that Wright's treatment is simple and univocal. Everyone knows that his ideas grow and span as does his organic architecture itself. So while the word "organic" means for him a function finding its proper form just as the oak or pine realizes through a period of development the shape appropriate to it, it also can imply the glory of a vigorous maturation. His own art is the flowering of an occasion, and he used the word "efflorescence" in referring to the achievement of Sullivan.[36] This means that his organic architecture, springing from its soil of conditions and needs, is not limited to a bare matching of those conditions. Rather, organic architecture here transcends the functional and efficient and rises into the bright manifestation of energy. What the seed produces, when matured in Wright's imagination, is rich and colorful—Aristotle's "supervenient perfection." Wright's architecture is, as we all know, romantic as well as functional; and the word "organic" covers both phases. Just as a tension revealed itself among the meanings of "clean," so a polarity comes to light here in the attempt to define architectural organicism. Architecture, organic in the sense of the crystal, freezes the individual thrust toward vital abundance. So it is part of the Soviet ideology to deny value to the individual work in its romantic isolation. But with another kind of organic architecture, transcending in bloom and joy its conditions, and rising from law into grace, we pass to our third variant.

In characterizing the architecture of the San Francisco Bay region, Lewis Mumford called it an "organic architecture which seems to have come about through unforced personal growth."[37] In her longer and more intimate essay Elisabeth Thompson finds this organic architecture earning the caption "vital."[38] "Vital" is in our list of the most used honorific terms. Gropius, for example, with his different Bauhaus orientation, is translated as employing the root term four times on one page.[39] Linked with the idea of organism in Bay Region architecture, it implies not only freshness, individuality, and creativity, but even historical continuity. Traditional architectural practice is not cut off from "modern" construction for this group of builders, but fertilizes it and gives it the sanction of good ancestry. The flowering of building on the bay included in its scope not only individual variation, sentiment for the intangibles of "home," but respect for the past.

Polarity shows itself, then, in organic architecture in the attitude toward the history of architecture. The moderns have been prone to be antihistorical. Indeed the first term on our list of favorite adjectives was "modern," and deservedly so; for the set of words characterizing and praising today's independent attitude of the new builders is more common than any other. They say they belong to the living present, directly affirm our contemporary world, are members of the new order, and so on. The purge that has accompanied their fastidious cleanliness has in general implied rejection of past architectural habits. In this respect the extreme is once more the Russian crystalline reform. For the Soviets right after the Revolution no continuity seemed possible. With life and economy made over on a new pattern, housing, clubs, bureaus, and industry had all to be cut *de novo*. But where there has been no such radical revolution, organic architecture would seem in principle to call for rooting in the past as well as flowering toward the future. For "the modern is never simple; it is always, so to speak, on the top of something else; always charged with a contradiction, with a reminiscence, in one word, with a history."[40]

In general, one can no more have an art that initiates its own world than one can perceive without apperceiving. What is created anew has always to be this or the other particular aspect. Even the crystalline Russian in the very midst of talk about *"nicht nur weiter verbessern, ausbauen, sondern ganz neu umbauen"* reports complacently Russian prefabrication in the seventeenth century, so that continuity, deeply imbedded, yet exists.

Writers who designate architecture as "organic" may then mean almost opposite things by the same word of praise, just as they may be intending diverse qualities by "clean." If Sense *3* of "organic," the concrete and historical, be grafted on to Sense *1* of "clean," an ideal of design tolerant of all good suggestion from history, locus, or feeling is welcomed without allowing irrelevance. Sense *4* of "clean" and Sense *1* of "organic" converge toward the fetish of omission, and carry what purports to be mathematical rigor in the direction of mystic nihilism.

NOTES

1. *Modern Architecture* (Princeton, 1931), Inside Back Cover.
2. *Ibid.*, p. 38.
3. *Ibid.*, p. 19.
4. *Ibid.*, p. 52.
5. *Ibid.*, p. 35.
6. (London, New York, 1932), p. 353.
7. *New World of Space* (New York, 1948), p. 66.
8. (New York, n.d.), p. v.
9. *An Introduction to Modern Architecture* (New York, 1947), p. 90.
10. *Ibid.*, p. 2.
11. *Architectural Record*, CI (May, 1947), 114.
12. (New York, 1944), p. 114.
13. Lewis Mumford, *The Culture of Cities* (New York, 1938), p. 408.
14. *Architecture and the Spirit of Man* (Cambridge, Mass., 1949) p. 123; also see all of chap. ix.
15. "Art and Democracy," *Magazine of Art*, XL (Feb., 1947), 76.
16. *Mechanization Takes Command* (New York, 1949), Part VII, pp. 629-712.

37

17. (Boston, 1948), pp. 282-88. The section begins: "If there is one thing for which America is famous and of which all Americans are proud, it is that standard of living which allegedly provides a bathroom for all of us."

18. *When the Cathedrals Were White* (New York, 1947), pp. 34, 216, 217.

19. Mumford, *op. cit.*, p. 416.

20. H. P. Berlage, *Gedanken über Stil in der Baukunst* (Leipzig, 1905), pp. 52, 53. Quoted by S. Giedion, *Space, Time and Architecture* (Cambridge, Mass., 1942), p. 234.

21. Mock, *op. cit.*, p. 114.

22. Walter Gropius, *The New Architecture and the Bauhaus*, trans. Shand (London, 1935), p. 56.

23. "Esthetics," *Architectural Forum*, LXXXIX (Nov., 1948), 143.

24. *Russland (Neues Bauen in der Welt, Bd. 1)* (Wien, 1930).

25. *Ibid.*, p. 9

26. *Ibid.*, p. 10.

27. *Ibid.*, p. 11.

28. *Ibid.*, p. 10.

29. Kasimir Malewitsch, *Die Gegenstandslose Welt* (München, 1927), p. 92.

30. The following reference to the Suprematists is taken from "A Note on the New Russian Poetry," by Louis Lozowick, which appeared in *Broom*, 1922: "... the Suprematists ... seek the 'zero point of art' and the Nothingists (Nitchevoki) ... seem to have found it. Before the revolution Krutchenych thought this admirable:

> Dir boor shtchill
> oobyeshtchoor
> skoom
> vy so boo
> rlez

and now Malyevitch thinks this superb:

> Oole Ele Lel Lee One Kon See An
> Onon Koree Ree Koazambe Moena Lezh
> Sabno Oratr Tulozh Koaleebee Blestore
> Teebo Orene Alazh

"These quotations are as cryptic in the Russian original as in the literal English transcription. The theory of the extreme poetic Left absolves the poet from the use of comprehensible language. The great Russian poet Tyutchev said:

A thought once expressed
Becomes a lie."

31. *Op. cit.*

32. *Op. cit.,* p. 52.

33. *New Vision and Abstract of an Artist* (rev. ed.; New York, 1949), p. 62.

34. (New York, n..d.), p. 177.

35. In "Canon," by Eric de Maré, *Architectural Review,* CV (Feb., 1949), 96.

36. Henry Hope gives meaning to the term when he says that in Sullivan's architecture ornament and decoration were the final expression of the function—"mobile, delicate and sumptuous."

37. "The Architecture of the Bay Region," *Domestic Architecture of the San Francisco Bay Region* (San Francisco Museum of Art, 1949).

38. "Backgrounds and Beginnings," *ibid.*

39. *Op. cit.,* p. 62.

40. Bernard Bosanquet, *A History of Aesthetic* (London, 1922), p. 323.

ARCHITECTURE

AND

THE POET

"ARCHITECTURE AND THE POET"
FIRST APPEARED AS A GUEST EDITORIAL IN
"THE JOURNAL OF THE AMERICAN
INSTITUTE OF ARCHITECTS"

I THINK of housing projects as inward-looking groups." When I encountered this sentence in Dean Joseph Hudnut's *Architecture and the Spirit of Man* my mind strained forward toward a statement I had been looking for in books and articles on modern architecture and had on the whole missed. What required saying is here, I thought. The author is reckoning with our need to withdraw from time to time and live and think by ourselves, and he handles it under the idea of the inward orientation in right building. He is reflecting on this human need with the intention of drawing its shape and devising its shell. He is saying that on the perimeter of housing units there are the filtering skins, the porches and terraces, the group meeting places, the gardens organized with inclosures, the wide windows; and in the interior there are the flexible sections for eating and sleeping and talking; and then as the subtle final control for a family's values and varied functions there is some "blessed uninvaded work-room" or some lovely peaceful atavistic *cave*.

But I was of course wrong. By being "focused towards

the center and away from the boundaries" Mr. Hudnut meant that housing projects "should have at their center some interests which are shared in common by all and which are expressed in structures or open spaces shared by all." The more I reflected the more I realized that my dashed expectation had been a lapse on my part rather than a right. For the author had made it perfectly clear pages earlier that he liked stir and was city-set and collective-minded. He had spread it on the pages of chapter xiii that it was by the city and not by the poetical solitude of country places that his mind was fed and fortified; that while poets give the city to the devil he gives it to God; and that the haven of his dreams is a little flat at the corner of Broadway and Forty-second Street. The shaping and placing of a poet's place would hardly occur to him as a primary requirement of his profession.

And yet in a way my expectation was natural. For while in general our functional architects do not study the virtues of contemplation and creation in seclusion or shape bedrooms and quiet workrooms, Mr. Hudnut himself has widened the concept of housing's uses almost to the spirit's farthest horizon. He has given it memory and a symbolic spire, for instance. As I read, I feel with joy and relief the sweep of his sympathies and tolerances.

But the poet is hardly in his picture. Now a poet may be thought of in the singular, or at any rate, in the well-defined class of which Walt Whitman and Shelley are examples. But this is not the poet whose claim to architectural consideration I am presenting. One knows little of the poetic habit who knows only a list of the makers of epics, dramatic poems, and lyrics. Poetic invention is an entire precious way of life, and it includes all kinds of creativeness. In it are those who like Petrarch crave to meditate in solitude, or like Descartes hatch their new geometries while lying late in bed, or like Pico della Mirandola acknowledge the melancholy temperament but claim also its genius for the investigation "of the highest and most secret things," or like Yeats nurse their dreams in guarded reverie and record that the poet's favorite symbol for his fit shell is the tower, or like Virginia Woolf attribute the sterility of woman in literature to the lack of *A Room of Her Own,* or like Hō-Jō-Ki make their little ten-feet-square huts for worship and music and reading.

This value of contemplation and creative imagination is the one which architects still do not seriously and altogether shape a space for. The gentle humanity which gives its due to history and sentiment bridles at ποίησις (poiesis). Why? Apparently because the poet seems not to know his place within a group. He carries momentum and in the wrong direction. He is setting toward an inclosed interior in the heart of the house or toward some secluded tower chamber, and dragging along congenial functions and beings with him. Isn't he tainted with introversion? Won't he stick his head in a hole?

For the basic postulate of the latest school of functional architects is the primacy of the social factor in human need. The words "private" and "peace" occur, but far less often than "sharing," "collective," "group," "communal" and "organic." Frank Lloyd Wright was a friend of country places and matters. But today architects are preoccupied with the truth that men have got to learn to live together or die. They are not so acutely aware of the equivalent truth that with the contemporary underlining of social planning and the ideal of psychological adjustment, man is fast losing the power to live with himself. If man is always in a group, he not only cannot cherish unique vision and capacities but he gets afraid of himself for a companion. Pejorative terms such as escapist and poet-conspirator betray this bias. It goes without saying that the city planners hate congestion and disorder in the life together. And Mr. Mumford even speaks of the "brutal lack of intimacy in most cities." His praise of such a collective housing development as Fresh Meadows is balanced by his persistent recurrence to the eternal ruminator in us all and his architectural needs. But by and large today's designers are little concerned with the poet's corner, the prophet's chamber, and the philosopher's armchair.

Contemporary architects not only focus on shared functions and space, but on these in our present era. Designing must be for the concerns of our age of speed, vast cities and dimensions, machines and techniques, political, economic, and social planning, the channeling of work to be done, and the organization of organizations. These comprise in truth the spirit of modernity. But architects have always, as we know, built in some sense in the spirit of their own modernity. One wonders how far they might now try to *maladjust* to their age in order to guide the indweller toward individual creativeness and thoughtfulness. Let us recall such a maladjustment upon which we can get the perspective of history.

In Greece there once lived a man named Socrates. His ways have made a difference to two thousand years of human experience. He was a lover of the city like Mr. Hudnut and made jokes about his awkwardness and naïveté when caught outside the walls. He "functioned" as an intellectual gadfly in the community center, in the "heart" of Athens. He used the downtown district for his ironical talk and pursuit of patterns of things. But the Socrates who philosophized and invented in the market place, public baths, and banquet rooms had previously ripened in himself by himself. He had odd rooms to do it in, I venture. But he could "participate" and "prick" because he had previously ingathered. One recalls his sudden withdrawals from company to live out a trance or hammer out an idea or entertain a vision. Then, and not till then, was he ready to co-operate. The intimacy of his mind was very far in indeed—farther in than the lovely village greens of ideal housing projects. The proper housing of Socrateses seems a worthy problem.

Being of the contemplative and poetical persuasion, I had thought of capping this essay: "I want a bedroom." But it seems better to bind it together in a graver and more general way, thus: Who has the imagination to design a proper place—study, bedroom, or penthouse—for the encouragement and protection of the imagination? If imagination is what "gives to airy nothings their local habitation," who will give a local habitation to imagination itself?

RECENT   POETS

ON

MAN   AND   HIS   PLACE

"RECENT POETS ON MAN AND HIS PLACE"
WAS DELIVERED AS THE PRESIDENTIAL ADDRESS
AT THE MEETING OF THE
AMERICAN PHILOSOPHICAL ASSOCIATION,
THE EASTERN DIVISION, AT YALE UNIVERSITY,
DECEMBER 27, 1946

O_{NE} OF THE founders of this association used to say: "The need for technical philosophy is small. But all things should be studied philosophically." This not only states clearly, in my opinion, the most frequent use of philosophy but hints at philosophy's best resource for her own continuing fruitful existence. In harmony with this view of philosophy's wider task, I have chosen for my theme the definition of essential traits in one art—poetry; in one period—the last half-century; and in one relation, viz., to the eternal philosophical problem of man and his place in the world.

Although to fix in definitions the nature of poetry and the arts has always been difficult, the great ones of our tradition have rarely failed to attempt it. Plato by no means failed to try, in spite of his fear of poetry's potency. Certainly Aristotle—Aristotle ancient and Aristotle medieval —brought a conspicuous kind of order into the field; for Aristotle ancient made of tragic poems a paradigm of necessary sequence, a symbolic revelation of probability; and Aristotle medieval framed cosmology on architecture.

Again, in that age when mathematical science most throve, Spinoza freed the imagination by noting its uncontending multifariousness and pictorial vividness, even before he wrote his philosophy *more geometrico;* and Leibniz, co-inventor of the calculus, almost fell into Pythagoras's danger of making the universe too musical. If, lately, some of our strict reasoners have warned their professional brethren to remain drily consequent if they would be honest, the gentle spectator of philosophers' careers has marked in several, who first agitated a philosophy strenuously scientific, a homecoming after a time to beauty and the arts for ampler truth. Have we not read in the later Whitehead: "Philosophy is the endeavour to find a conventional phraseology for the vivid suggestiveness of the poet"? And he who now represents us among the scientists argues in his latest discourse for the indispensable aesthetic component in an adequate world view.

On the whole philosophers have been not so much unmindful of the importance of poetry as impatient with its detail and suspicious of its nimble wit and far ranging. To be sure, virtual papers of separation have sometimes been drawn up. At such times pure philosophers and poets have made a convenient compact as to the duty of each. Poetry is what it is, according to this understanding, by its clean detachment from fact, and free fancy. Its function is restorative, image-forming, and beguiling, but not instructive. Science and philosophy are, according to this view, the authorities on verifiable knowledge, and the assumptions and relations involved. Now to such an understanding, the objection is: Only the developing history of the human spirit can show what in their courses poetry and philosophy are and do. The systematic distinction of functions, though necessary, draws lines where none exist in nature. Certainly much poetry moves in "faërie" and "nothing affirmeth, and therefore never lieth." But no eternal law prohibits to poetry concern with facts and general ideas. At any rate, in the past fifty years, poets have appeared to intend many satirical comments on the surrounding state of affairs. Not only within their shaggy verses have they passed judgment on the society in which they live, but they have used philosophical sanctions for their judgments. Plato's ghost is invoked by one to serve as a chorus to scoff at such of our fellow citizens as are throughout life "perfectly adjusted"; Socrates's ghost, by another, to sustain the hope that we do not know what we think we know when we look around us. Still another threads a lament over the decay of human dignity and passion upon the symbol of Heraclitean fire. More significant than words and names, however, is the tone and intention. In the midst of his poet's *Note-Book,* Paul Valéry suddenly says: "I was wishing to speak of philosophers —and to philosophers." What he had on his mind was to suggest that philosophers might profit in their capacity to express their ideas exactly by submitting themselves to the severe discipline of poetical composition. He implies that they are insufficiently aware of the fine relations of language to thought, and of the interaction of the parts of language with each other. This then is a contribution poetry feels itself competent to make to philosophy. But it is not of philosophy's need of poetry that William Butler Yeats talks. In his late prose writings he recurs more than once to the absorption of philosophy by poetry in the period between 1920 and 1930. In the twenties, he says, the poets put into their poems a sense of suffering that was no longer passive, "no longer an obsession of the nerves," but one that "philosophy had made a part of all the mind." And Hopkins, the poet who—born before his time—by common consent has influenced our contemporary poets most, insists upon the engagement with reality, seriousness, as the proper virtue of right poetry. "A kind of touchstone of the highest or most living art is seriousness," he says, "not gravity, but the being in earnest with your subject . . . reality."

Quotations from recent poetry which contain such words as "reality" and "seriousness" and reporting "the sudden return of philosophy into English literature about 1925" do not of course establish in themselves kinship with what philosophers themselves understand by "reality" and "philosophy." A poet's employment of these terms, even if Valéry is right in claiming for them superior subtlety, would cause a use both more concrete and symbolic than professional sorters of facts and ideas would often approve. The Heraclitus of the hearthstone and liturgical torch is not the Heraclitus among the cosmologists. But this stricture does not affect the special claim of our argument here. Though recent poets have sometimes used verse for general reflection, on the whole it is by an intensification of their own special habits that poets offer suggestion to philosophy and touch its borders by fruitful contrast or supplementation. We must agree that the moving power of poetry can only seem relevant to strict philosophical reflection if it can somehow be placed by reason in a world where reason orders. But we intend to maintain the paradox, even so, that the new style, whatever the roughness of its manner and apparent madness of its moods, is the outer sign of a new inner seriousness and intense engagement with reality. We are to hold that our poetry has been dense and incoherent in recent years partly because its authors have suffered from the world and have in turn bitten into it to an unusual degree, and have made this double interplay the fuel and shaper of song. This same double phenomenon—acting and being acted on—can appear, we remember, in the far recesses of metaphysical discussion as a candidate for "mark of being."

We said just now that the contemporary poet's relevance to the philosopher was largely the result of an intensification of the poet's traditional habits. What are these habits?

The poet's way of behaving Milton called "sensuous and passionate." Poetry, he would say, is more immediate than thought, closer to the impact on eye and ear of color and sound; and that inside the poet the reverberations of these fresh impacts still are preserved and mingle in his song. But along with this "heat" of the poet, Croce has placed the contrary quality: "coldness." Croce means that when the poet works as artist he maintains a certain aloofness from his kind and the world about him, and acknowledges no law but that of his own craft.

That there is a deep paradox in the poet's nature many have recently noted. I shall only be putting my own interpretation and mode of expression on a common observation when I draw out what the paradox seems to me in part to be, and what its use for us.

The poet belongs to the class of sensitive beings. Whatever goes on around him, or echoes within, finds him attentive beyond the average. He is finely aware, but he is also strongly aware. His mode of taking impressions suggests to the onlooker something like physical disturbance, or at least visible excitation. One recent poet has said of all poets that their particular faculty is to receive vibrations and transmit them. "Vibration," "trembling," "throbbing," "pulsing"—these words are noticeably frequent in descriptions of the way the poet is affected by experience. When the stimulus reaches the limit of its importance for him, he is said to be in ecstasy—that is, moved out of position. All these metaphors bear witness to the delicacy with which the poet's nerves are swung and the ease with which they are deflected.

But it is no less striking a fact about the class of beings called poets, that they are the origin of impresses received by other things. Indeed, unless a poet has energy enough to plant a shape he wills on what he treats for the time being as mere stuff—mere potentiality of existence—he is no poet. Sometimes we call this side of the poet's nature the artist or craftsman in the poet. But that is quibbling, for the word "poet" itself means maker. Unless the poet shows himself, from one point of view, as first cause of permanently delectable aesthetic effects from measured language—even suggesting divinity in his power of making and unmaking waves of air and chance impressions—we classify him as a man of sensibility only. An epigrammatic definition of the imagination stamped out by Gerard Manley Hopkins—"the imagination is the hand within the mind" —is token of the fact that a poet more molds sensation than collects it. In general, we now suggest, the poet is the doer-and-undergoer, par excellence.

The doubleness of the poet shines out in his relation to his two chief pieces of equipment: images and rhythm. Are they presents to him, or does he construct them? Both. The musical alternation of rhythm, by his own testimony,

is the effectual afterimage, in his pulses and interior con-
versation, of the advance and recession of waves upon the
shore, swaying of boughs in the wind, or other rocking
thing in nature or his own processes. But to this origin in
the end goes less than half the credit. If the swinging of
wind and waves or hands and feet is born again as thesis
and arsis, caesura and phrase, the imagination's "hand
within the mind" gives what so comes its final form. Poets
put into a kind of inner laboratory of cadences and balances those little tunes that they find singing themselves
within. Their cunning devises tricks of acceleration and
retardation and sudden shifts of melody to impress an idea,
as thus:

> And for darkened Man, that complex multiplicity
> Of air and water, plant and animal,
> Hard diamond; infinite sun.

The whole puzzling paradox of where rhythm comes from
is debated by Wallace Stevens in his "Idea of Order at
Key West." Of a singer making music by the sea he writes:

> It may be that in all her phrases stirred
> The grinding water and the gasping wind.

i.e., nature furnishes part of the cause. But the human
act, and articulate language, he immediately adds, are a
larger part.

> But it was she and not the sea we heard.
> She sang beyond the genius of the sea.
> The song and water were not medleyed sound
> Since what she sang was uttered word by word.

He puts his finger on the human motivation when he says
that the maker, man, has a passion to order, with his language, the words of the sea.

On the semantic side, the poet's material is imagery. Here also there is ambiguity, for imagery seems lately to have moved both closer to and further away from reality. On the whole the recent poets' images have deepened into symbols. The tendency to depict the lovable shows of nature by delicate comparisons, while always with us, has yielded in large measure to adumbrations through imagery less sensuous and more reflective of hidden forms. Or rather, imagery's mode has split itself into the full compass of possible contradiction. The symbol is designed to tell some kind of serious truth about the bottom of the soul or the naked twentieth century. Yeats has noted the pervasiveness in recent verse of the symbol "bone" and remarks that the image of the "star" flourished in an earlier time. He attaches meaning to this shift, and certain it is that not for nothing have unhappy figures of deserts and carrion, filth and asses, thickened on the poets' pages. But while images are used thus starkly to convey with force the nature of our ugly environment, the poet is also more than commonly concerned with a symbol's intrinsic, half-drunken multifariousness. He uses fantastic forms, as if he were engineering a ballet. Indeed, part of the obscurity of recent poetry comes from its double aim, to wit: both analysis of reality into essential meanings, and also a delighted tumbling about with the possible multiple suggestions of words as such. Nonsense and a sybil's wisdom seem both to be courted. The poet, says Stevens, in *Notes Toward a Supreme Fiction,* went into the park, sat down on a bench, and passed into the poet's trance. The lake in front of him became his

> Theatre of trope . . .
> The water of

> The lake was full of artificial things,
> Like a page of music, like an upper air,
> Like a momentary color, in which swans
> Were seraphs, were saints, were changing essences.

In the trance, the poet continues, metaphor became a kind of irresponsible vagabond, that made "iris frettings on the blank." Yet a favorite emphasis in Stevens is the danger of anthropomorphic thinking.—Again the same poet who, exulting in aesthetic freedom, wrote,

> Gather me
> Into the artifice of eternity . . .
> I shall never take
> My bodily form from any natural thing
> But such a form as Grecian goldsmiths make
> Of hammered gold and gold enameling . . .

also wrote:

> Parnell came down the road, he said to a cheering
> man:
> Ireland shall get her freedom and you shall break
> stones.

A third example: The same poet who seemed to send forth her mesmeric lines,

> Monotonously fell the rain
> Like thoughts within an empty brain

for whatever suggestion the sound and symbol could evoke, found the same image crystallizing itself to stand for the raids on London in 1940:

> Still falls the Rain—
> Dark as the world of man, black as our loss.

We have been saying that poetry, born in the vibration of its inspiration, sustained in wavering rhythms and ambiguous symbols, is always characterized by double or plural pointing, even to the height of its completest communication. Indeed, it often prospers best if its residual meaning strains against nature, making two great faces of things confront each other and strike fire for the imagination through their friction. In other words, important poetic fiction may by its apparent intense unreason throw light on those metaphysical first principles that Whitehead says "mutely appeal for an imaginative leap." Those early metaphysical poets with whom the moderns feel so close a kinship conveyed their meaning by daring conjunctions and vast alternatives, as: lust and religion, Heaven and Hell, woman-angel and woman-Eve, the universe and the bridal bed.—Donne wrote·

> She's all States, and all Princes, I,
> Nothing else is.

The reflective and disturbed poets of the twentieth century draw their multiple meaning and vast alternatives mostly from what the twentieth century or the recent past presents to them. Even when they veil their meaning in old Greek or Irish myths, the tenor is often contemporary. Inspecting these poems, we find burdening their course the oppositions of war and peace, dead culture and eternal salvation, socialism and capitalism, tyranny and freedom. But we also find properly metaphysical problems: the relation of time to eternity, the bounded object to space, and—our own problem in this paper—man to his world. "What can man do?" "How effectual is man's will?" "How far is man creature and in what sense creator of his world?" These questions sound familiar to philosophers. Examination of recent poetry reveals their presence there.

Recent Poets on Man and His Place

Sometimes the problematic situation of man in his world is stated plainly, as in W. H. Auden's:

> We are created from and with the world
> To suffer with and from it day by day:
> Whether we meet in a majestic world
> Of solid measurements or a dream world
> Of swans and gold . . .
> Our claim to own our bodies and our world
> Is our catastrophe. What can we know
> But panic and catastrophe until we know
> Our dreadful appetite demands a world
> Whose order, origin, and purpose will
> Be fluent satisfaction of our will.

Plain putting of the question is frequent in Wallace Stevens. In fact he seems half-consciously to debate the claims of man, the natural reflex of his environment, versus man, source of his experiences and shaper of his history. The first claim is the theme of the half-humorous tiny poem "Theory";

> I am what is around me.
> Women understand this.
> One is not a duchess
> A hundred yards from a carriage.
>
> These, then, are portraits:
> A black vestibule,
> A high bed sheltered by curtains.

In general, Stevens is fond of saying that men are nothing more than "invisible elements of places made visible."

> The soul, he said, is composed
> Of the external world.
> The man in Georgia walking among pines
> Should be pine-spokesman.

But Stevens does, even so, impute a very powerful imaginative faculty to his earthy men: he writes:

> the mind
> Turns to its own figurations and declares,
> This image, this love, I compose myself of these
> As in the powerful mirror of my wish and will.

When abstract questions appear baldly in their verses, poets are not usually at their best. But the way recent poets have expressed through images human suffering, and at the same time reached after some faith in and way of conceiving human power, makes, in the interaction of the two, a clear call to the thinker's ordering function. How can the sorter of ideas reconcile Hopkins's man: "soft sift in an hour-glass" with Stevens's: "the doer of all that angels can" and "crystallizer of the revolving world"? The problem is admittedly universal and eternal. Older poets have aired it in their manner. But the new poets, introspective and rebellious, have often carried both their problem and their technique into the ferment of the soul's "dark night." Their style and thinking have been aptly described by Yeats: "constantly interrupted, broken, twisted into nothing by its direct opposite, . . . [qualified by] nervous obsession, nightmare, stammering conclusion . . . loss of self-control . . . unbridged transitions, unexplained ejaculations, that make [the] meaning unintelligible."

I have chosen to analyze the suggestions of these difficult poets, as they bear on our main problem, under three symbolic captions: (1) Man, the puppet. I draw here from Thomas Hardy. (2) Man, the cutter of agate. The phrase is Yeats's. (3) Man, the leaping laugher. This is the title of a poem by George Barker. These three categories stand for various ways in which man is active and passive in his world. My first source, Thomas Hardy, is relatively simple. In him, man is passive—even worse, a puppet.

Thomas Hardy published *The Dynasts* in 1903. In the Preface he states that the poem was shaped to give a "modern expression of a modern outlook." What he takes the "modern outlook" to be he describes a little further on. "The meditative world," he says, "is older, more invidious, more nervous, more quizzical, than it once was, and . . . unhappily perplexed by—Riddles of Death Thebes never knew."

He chooses for the expression of these unhappy perplexities certain Phantom Intelligences that he domiciles in an Overworld. From this unearthly perspective the Ancient Spirit of the Years, the Spirit of the Pities, and the Spirits Sinister and Ironic comment through their dramatic choruses on the Napoleonic wars. Hardy is a vivid chronicler. Some of the scenes of the historical pageant, such as that of the death of Nelson on the "Victory" at Trafalgar and of common British soldiers dying in dark cellars in Spain, no reader is likely to forget. Yet it is not so much with the desperate human interest of these characters, actions, passions, and events that Hardy is ultimately concerned as with their record on the high balance sheet of the Phantom Intelligences. For Hardy as for Aristotle, tragedy, though an imitation of the actions and passions of men, is more serious and philosophical than history. He like Aristotle is interested in the element of necessity present in human affairs. He ruminates the riddle of predicates of value.

The comments from the Overworld, as they issue now from the Spirit of the Years who is the spokesman of the clock-like Mechanism at the Back of Things, and now from the Spirits of Pity and Irony, are logically incompatible, as dramatic statements have a right to be. But there is a flash in the collision of Hardy's Mechanism and Humanism as if from the broken colors in Impressionist painting. On the one hand, values are made nonexistent. The Universe is an automaton

> Unweeting why or whence.
> It works unconsciously . . .
> Eternal artistries in Circumstance . . .
> > the pulsion of the Byss
>
> . . . .
> Unchecks its clock-like laws.
> . . . The systems of the suns go sweeping on . . .
> In mathematic roll unceasingly . . . .

Or, as Hardy's metaphors accumulate, the universe is "a sublime fermenting-vat," "a knitter drowsed," "a viewless, voiceless, Turner of the Wheel." It is obviously nonsense to speak of good or evil in such a context. On the other hand, Pity not only assigns at the outset a value—a negative one—to all terrestrial history, but at times breaks into the earthly scene, e. g., to protest in Napoleon's ear his treachery to the cause of Liberty, or to ask for the merciful *coup de grâce* for wounded soldiers crazed, blaspheming, and in agony. The Spirits Ironical and Sinister, though less Heart and more Intellect than the Spirit of Pity, collide even more effectively with the World Mechanism. Pity is indeed made "loving-kind" by Hardy but also young and ineffectual. Pity chants a vague, melancholy sentiment at the beginning of the Poem:

> We would establish those of kindlier build,
> In fair Compassions skilled,

> The mild, the fragile, the obscure content. . . .
> Those, too, who love the true, the excellent,
> And make their daily moves a melody.

And she voices another vague, sweet wish at the end:

> that the rages
> Of the ages
> Shall be cancelled,
> Consciousness the Will informing, till It fashions
> all things fair.

The Spirits Sinister and Ironical on the other hand are powers with cutting edges. Their remarks shock us because the more the Tale becomes humanly tragic, the more it feeds their dramatic intelligences with food for laughter. Pity, grieved past bearing, cries that she cannot bear the beacons of war lit on Egdon Heath, but Spirit Sinister says:

> This is good, and spells blood. I assume that It means to let us carry out this invasion with pleasing slaughter, so as not to disappoint my hope?

and after a few minutes makes this generalization: "My argument is that War makes rattling good history; but Peace is poor reading. So I back Bonaparte for the reason that he will give pleasure to posterity." When the Spirit of Pity says of General Mack before Ulm, "The clouds weep for him," Spirit Sinister answers:

> If he must he must;
> And it's good antic at a vacant time.

If one now inquires: What place does man occupy in Hardy's universe, one would be tempted to answer first: "A place on a puppet's stage. In other words, no place." Hardy himself uses the metaphor of puppets for his characters and the pulling of wires for their actions. But he also lets his Phantom Intelligences call attention to the intolerable contradiction "of making figments feel,"

> that they feel, and puppetry remain
> Is an owned flaw in [Nature's] consistency.

So the second answer is: Man appears in Hardy's world as the sufferer. The poet, we said at the beginning, is acutely sensitive to the impressions moving in on him from the natural and human world. Hardy is such a sensitive; he so vibrates; he so makes us vibrate by his imaginative vision of the victims of the Napoleonic wars. If now we change our position, taking Hardy with us, from drama to orderly and consistent philosophy, we must say: It cannot be both ways. Suffering is not a mechanical event. Either the universe is different, or man is different from Hardy's picturing. We can say more: Though Hardy's characters suffer and Hardy must have had parallel feelings in construing his scenes, Hardy has been a powerful maker in the process of building his puppet show. A man who can originate such a momentous spectacle is not a passive creature in a fermenting vat. He is what every great poet is, an amazing agent. He was not fitted to picture rebels, nor actuate on his stage the morally responsible soul. But such beings are implications of Hardy's own functioning.

With the arrival of our second phase—man, the cutter of agate, the fine craftsman—our subject becomes more complicated. The artist in the poet now swells almost to the point of crowding out the physical and historical man in his human environment. The "place" of the poet's concern is his own workbench.

"The chief use of the meaning of a poem," says T. S.

Eliot, "is to keep the [reader's] mind diverted and quiet, while the poem does its work upon him; much as the imaginary burglar is always provided with a bit of nice meat for the house-dog." Eliot is speaking of only one class of poet. But this class has lately been conspicuous. The business of such a poet, Eliot is here suggesting, is to polish his instrument and discipline his hand, using a recognizable subject only as a concession to our habitual un-fineness. When Eliot uses the expression "while the poem does its work upon him," he apparently means: "while the poet awakens the reader's pure sensitivity." Concentrated incantation is always part of what a poet does and may be all. Listen to Paul Valéry: "The thought must be hidden in verse as nutritive virtue is hidden in fruit. Fruit is nourishment, though it seems to be nothing but delight. One perceives only pleasure; and yet one receives a substance—Enchantment—*that* is the nourishment conveyed to one. And sweet is its going down" ("Le passage est suave").

The implementation of this *suave passage* is, then, in the belief of the delicate carvers of verbal agates, the poet's main task. Interest in texture, rhythm, pattern, and structure for the moment outweighs interest in objective reference. The new group have adopted a new principle of metrical equivalence which supplants for them the simple old way of measuring feet by counting off equal numbers of syllables, somewhat as the far subtler nuclear physics has made obsolete the older theory of atomic substances. According to the principle of metrical equivalence, the cadence and balance of verse depend in part on a fine, felt awareness of the pressures and resistances of nuanced vowels and operated consonants, labials, and sibilants. Here is an example of slow movement, sibilants, thin vowels: "A mouth like old silk soft with use." In:

> Like gript stick
> Still I sit

there are sibilants and thin vowels, but the vowels are tightly wrapped in difficult consonants, and there is effort in movement. Texture is interwoven with subtly counter-pointed rhythm so that the total metrical pattern becomes rich and varied, almost to the confounding of old reading habits, as in the following:

> He comes among
> The summer throngs of the young
> Rose, and in his long
> Hands flowers, fingers, carries;
> Dreamed of like aviaries
> In which many phoenixes sing,
> Promising touch soon
> In summer, never to come.

Rhyme is often in the middle of lines, instead of tapping off conclusions, and the delicious near-rhyme pleases these poets more than full echo.

On grounds of harmony and proportion—and lack of verifiable meaning—Valéry classifies Pascal's famous line "Le Silence éternel de ces espaces infinis M'EFFRAYE" ("The eternal Silence of these infinite spaces frightens me") as a "perfect poem"—not a "thought," as it is classified by its author. Here, says Valéry, is rhetorical symmetry; a formidable metaphor of equilibrium: the noun "silence" balances the noun "spaces"; the adjective "eternal," the second adjective "infinite"; again, this whole massive characterization of the cosmos is set in contrast to its little human offshoot, in the short verbal sign of his terror: "M'EFFRAYE."

The creation of enchantment by formal devices may go so far as the creation of an artificial universe. This is precisely what Valéry claims for the quoted "Pensée" of Pascal. "This vast verse," he says, "constructs the rhetorical image of a system complete in itself, a Universe." Here is that supersensuous body that imagination's rhythms and timbres engender. The carved agate, the beautiful crystal, thus slips into the place vacated by common subject, common meaning, man and his world.

The airy affinities of this delicate workmanship are mathematics and music. In such fields grow harmonious fictions whose validity is not measured in terms of common experience. Our poets often use the musical analogy, as in

> a vivid apprehension . . .
> In an interior ocean's rocking
> Of long, capricious fugues and chorals.

and:

> the study of the music
> Of *Ash-Wednesday* should compel the minds of all
> Poets; for in a hundred years no poem
> Has sung itself so exquisitely well.

Poetry's linkage with music reminds us that "elliptical," oblique, unearthly poetry may, like music, have symbolic meaning. And the question arises whether symbols may give a richer content and suggestiveness than more familiar representation can. The fact that "subject" is thrown to the common reader like a piece of meat by the burglar to the house dog does not exclude a symbol's "evocation." If one then asks what is the deliverance of "evocation" on the problem of "Man and His Place," the answer proves to be less tenuous than one at first thought. Of course "evoked" meanings are not convertible into factual propositions. They stir up sentiments and actuate moods. The words "eternal" and "infinite," says Valéry, as he develops his analysis of Pascal's "perfect little poem," "are symbols of non-thought. Their value is wholly affective. . . . They provoke the particular sensation of the impotence of imagining." But there is more in some recent poetical music than sensation and affective value, or a kernel of vague enchantment. There is a kind of semantic revenge, or public meaning-in-spite-of-intention. The subject that pervades a considerable body of this delicately carved poetry is the ruin of our present civilization by greed and worldly ambition. Flashing across the dark picture are nostalgic memories of the author's own childhood. In their search for the rightly weighted set of sounds and the rhythms counterpointed and wavering, our enchanters confess that —at least in part—they look deep within themselves as they pass into lyricism. There they find not only little tunes, and an urge for swinging, varied balance, but flickering scenes, memorable because of blissful, irresponsible playdays.

In Eliot's "Burnt Norton," for example, after a few solemn lines, without any explicit bridge there comes this:

> Footfalls echo in the memory
> Down the passage . . .
> Towards the door . . .
> Into the rose-garden. My words echo
> Thus, in your mind.

Then we get a faint reference to birds, rose leaves, a pool, laughter—then:

Go, said the bird, for the leaves were full of children
Hidden excitedly, containing laughter.

At the end, in symmetry, there is the same dim recalling of childish games in the rose garden. Except for bright reliefs like this, the "subject" runs on the surrounding vulgarity and spiritual death. Man's place for many an agate-cutter is a pessimist's chaos, ugly, selfish, obscene. Its west has declined; its values are decadent. It is a "rat's alley," "stony rubbish," "a heap of broken images." The inhabitants of "The Waste Land" are "hooded hordes swarming" over endless plains, stumbling in cracked earth. Individually they are palmists, scented with synthetic perfumes, toothless whores, drowned and having their bones picked, lean solicitors reading last testaments. Man and his place is here—dust-to-dust. Eliot reveals his core of feeling in *The Waste Land* when he says: "I will show you fear in a handful of dust." Edith Sitwell calls man's place a "spider's universe,"—"the idiot drum of a universe changed to a circus."

The problem that the agate-cutter sets for the consistency-loving philosopher is, in our present context, this: The poet, as refiner of language, finds his tool both instrument of enchantment (the functioning of language here being at the same time language as intrinsic value) and instrument of satire, fit to scorch our world. He makes a world of his own which is music; he uses that music to tell off contemporary manners. The resultant effect is that simultaneous tension of hating and loving such as Sappho and Catullus ascribe to the distracted lover. In the behavior of these poets as I have interpreted it, there seems to be a maximum of contradictory attitudes; a repudiation of a beastly world and the fine evocation of a world of carved autonomous beauty. The location of the behavior betrays, I think, the source of the contradiction. Both in doing and undergoing, these poets transact, by and large, with surfaces. Fastidious sensibilities as they essentially are, they recoil at once from filth and greed as they see it in its outward shows, and they make, for their consolation, exquisite textures, which are also word surfaces that they tend to caress with the sensitive surface of their imagination's hand. Both the doing and the undergoing are nervously energetic but plastically inhibited, because of the immediacy of the reaction; one might without too much exaggeration say that the poet remains suspended, vibrating, between what comes into him and what goes out from him. Is a philosopher prepared to say that if the poet's theme is the world around him, and without him, he takes it inadequately when his references are typically pejorative? Does such a poet perhaps not know incisively and thoroughly the good side of essential humanity? If he both felt and worked with a larger part of himself and deeper layers of his place, would both the tone and the reference of his poetry change?

Although the contradiction of the Hardyesque mood is gone (man made a puppet by a man who is anything but a puppet), still a degree of the passivity of Hardy's attitudes survives. The poet of our second type is still too impressionable for one whose calling is "making."

Yeats wrote "The Cutting of an Agate" between 1903 and 1915. He then declared that he hoped to have got far enough away from life to "make credible strange events and elaborate words." He came back to life about 1925 along with many other poets who, as he tells us, awoke in that day to a sense of their responsibility. On Christmas day, 1936, he wrote:

I am an old man now and month by month my capacity and energy must slip away, so what is the use of saying that both in England and Ireland I want to stiffen the backbone of the high-hearted and high-minded and the sweet-hearted and sweet-minded, so that they may no longer shrink and hedge, when they face rag-merchants like **X**. Indeed before all I want to strengthen myself. It is not our business to reply to this and that, but to set up our love and indignation against their pity and hate.

Here the poet assumes a moral duty: to stiffen the backbone of the spiritually distinguished by the diffusion of joy based on a vision of truth. But what the poet's work is, once he has become a brother of the common life, may easily be confused by him and by others. He is to diffuse joy, but as only he can, and with a new emotional accent. The poet's place in the world is still the place of the poet, even if the poet claims participation in what concerns us all. He is still the explorer and master of language, the speaker of "imagination's Latin," even if his language aims at wider relevance. In *"Esthétique du mal,"* Wallace Stevens, conning over man's ills, asserts in a setoff distich that our savior, in this plight, is the music of language:

> Natives of poverty, children of malheur
> The gaiety of language is our seigneur.

Indeed it is by remaining poet that the poet best fights for his country. Stevens says:

> The soldier is poor without the poet's lines,
> His petty syllabi, the sounds that stick
> Inevitably modulating, in the blood.
> And war for war, each has its gallant kind.
> How simply the fictive hero becomes the real;
> How gladly with proper words the soldier dies,
> If he must, or lives on the bread of faithful speech.

I mentioned earlier that the modern poet has offered

his practical services to the philosopher for instruction in the sharpening of speech. Workers with words have a good housekeeper's revulsion against messiness in verbal indication. A recent poet has said that public life would benefit if our legislators could achieve something like verbal-surgical cleanliness through the emulation of poetic practice. The suggestion that language is bread for the soldier and surgical instrument for the statesman has the advantage of implying that words are more than signs and symbols. It emphasizes their common use and makes them a kind of thing in the world of things. But teaching philosophers and lawmakers how to read and write is still an avocation of the poet, rather than his vocation.

"Illumination of plain and common things," one poet suggests, is the work of the poet, false romanticism having now been dismissed. So he sings about "Ploughing on Sunday," and "Lilacs in Carolina," "Two Pears," and "A Glass of Water." Another poet asks poets in the same vein: "Are we, perhaps, here just for saying:

> House,
> Bridge, Fountain, Gate, Jug, Olive tree, Window, —
> possibly: Pillar, Tower? . . . but for saying, remember,
> oh, for such saying. . . .

As Americans I think we may congratulate ourselves on the success of our poets in this kind. We celebrate with felicity the homely things in our landscape: stone walls, birch trees, and subways. It proves that the salt of lightness seasons our poetical feasts, and that we know the high value of democratic conviviality—living with things around us on gay terms. If Democritus's Ghost would protect me, I would even suggest that a more literal kind of conviviality is a holiday invocation of the poet:

Noah he often said to his wife when he sat down to dine
I don't care where the water goes if it doesn't get
into the wine.

Yeats listed "humorous self-forgetful drunkenness" and
mischievousness, along with physical beauty and courage,
among "beautiful lofty things."

My father upon the Abbey stage, before him a raging
   crowd.
"This Land of Saints," and then as the applause died out,
"Of Plaster Saints," his beautiful mischievous head thrown
   back.
Standish O'Grady supporting himself between the tables
Speaking to a drunken audience high nonsensical words;
Augusta Gregory seated at her great ormulu table
Her eightieth winter approaching: "Yesterday he threat-
   ened my life,
I told him that nightly from six to seven I sat at this table,
The blinds drawn up."

This transition from nonsense to courage brings us
back to Yeats's pronouncement: that the work of the poet
as distinctive agent in the common world is to stiffen the
backbone of the spiritually minded by the diffusion of
joy based on a vision of truth. The mood required is that
of a curious double-edged laughter, laughter that attacks
as well as rejoices.

You remember Kant's definition of laughter: expectation suddenly brought to nothing, the traumatic collapse of
psychic habit setting up a spasmodic vibration of the dia-
phragm. If we may be pardoned violence to Kant's for-
mula we may say: Poetic generation as leaping laughter
is here and now ordinary expectation suddenly brought to
something, to dangerous lyrical potency, the collision
setting up a trembling of the whole man. For a poet's

laughter, on this view, "completes the partial mind" and marks an access of energy that spreads over the entire organism. *Poiesis* often signalizes a moment of excited discovery. There is a sudden discontinuity when the poet strikes in and makes his fertile encounter. With Louis McNeice, he exclaims, "The world is suddener than we think it." His insights, Wallace Stevens says, are

> moments of awakening
> Extreme, fortuitous, personal, in which
> We more than awaken, sit on the edge of sleep,
> As on an elevation.

This laughing poetry crowns discovery with "sudden glory" and acts both as release and recharge. The poet is all at once aware that he can triumph over the toughest, hardest material: his own inertia, if he is old,

> . . . My temptation is quiet,
> Here at life's end . . .
> Grant me an old man's frenzy . . .
> An old man's eagle mind;

—his own ambition, if he fancies himself important,

> Ambition is my death. That flat thin flame
> I feed, that plants my shadow;

his fear of his own body, if he has never felt at home in it; the rough, cruel world, if he recognizes his tendency toward oversensitivity,

> Many men mean
> Well: but tall walls
> Impede, their hands bleed and
> They fall, their seeds the
> Seed of the fallen . . .
>
> Whom the noonday washes

> Whole, whom the heavens compel
> And to whom pass immaculate messages . . .

> Impede impediments
> Leap mountains, laugh at walls.

But the double edge of the laughter implies contrary
moods as well as collision of a poet with his weakness and
his world. Irony and bitterness, sometimes vulgar, defiant
riotousness, pull against complaisance and gaiety. Yeats,
in a memorable passage, claims for today's poetic laughter
a component of savage triumph that recalls Hobbes's conception. He quotes the saying of Swift, "When I am told
that somebody is my brother protestant, I remember that
the rat is a fellow creature," and comments: "That seems
to me a joyous saying." Now we delight in this example;
but when Yeats introduces a more sinister element in a
quotation from a Dutch mystic we are startled. The mystic
said: "I must rejoyce, I must rejoyce without ceasing,
though the whole world shudder at my joy." What kind
of joy is it, I ask, that causes universal shuddering? A joy, I
answer, whose energy has passed beyond the control of
reason. And yet, if reason is the function in man which
we believe directed toward objective report and actual
fact, it is reason which is immediately associated by Yeats
with the Dutch mystic's joy. These emotions, he says, do
not desire to change their object. They are "a form of
eternal contemplation of what is."

I think the philosopher may question whether the rejoicing poetry of today, in becoming active, acknowledges
any more the contemplative virtues. Practical in a sense
the new poets are; engaged actively with the world they
would be; and also aware of world-wide, deep-set human
problems, but too engrossed in their rich ambiguous re-

77

joicing for the difficult "contemplation of what is." They
sometimes confuse, I think, predilection for the palpable,
and a "large, loud liberty," with truth-telling, and dis-
missal of traditional belief with sense of fact. Ashamed of
an earlier fastidiousness, they have adopted a complemen-
tary one and so remain in their own way unobjective.
Two examples must suffice: the grosser aspects of life are
not only given their proportionate place but the protrud-
ing foreground—a baroque thrust, and the moral attitude
of compassion tends to be frowned on as weak. Yeats's
prayer secured for him, I think, his "old man's eagle mind."
All must acknowledge the lusty power of his late verse.
Out of what does song grow? he asks, and answers: "Five
things: the virgin, the harlot, the lion, the eagle, and the
wild." Here the statement is powerful, but balanced. But
he is too harsh when he writes that his inspiration is

> A mound of refuse or the sweepings of a street,
> Old kettles, old bottles, and a broken can,
> Old iron, old bones, old rags, that raving slut
> Who keeps the till. Now that my ladder's gone,
> I must lie down where all the ladders start,
> In the foul rag-and-bone shop of the heart.

Again, it is neither the virgin nor the harlot that Wallace
Stevens's poet yearns for, but

> the most grossly maternal, the creature
> Who most fecundly assuaged him, and not the mauve
> *Maman*. His anima liked its animal
> And liked it unsubjugated.

"Mauve *Maman*" is here perverse, I think. Again: Granted
that Auden is right in his commentary on "The Tempest"
in redeeming the unfairly treated Caliban and setting him

beside delicate Ariel, even so, on the whole, one hears too much of "earth's frankly brutal drum."

You will recall that Thomas Hardy, our first great poetical example, represented the spirit of pity as young and ineffectual; but yet he knew it deserved a place among the heavenly intelligences. What the new poets intend to do with pity is well expressed by Auden, when he says:

> . . . it is precisely in its negative image
> of Judgment that we can positively envisage Mercy.

Mercy—compassion—pity—this class of emotional attitudes seems, to these writers as it did to Spinoza, a lack of perfection, a failure in active virtue. The detached attitude of judging facts and values, or the ebullient one of rejoicing and so triumphing, is substituted. In Spender's phrase, "pity is the same as cruelty," because it turns life into water. He laughs at it with bitter satire:

> To the hanging despair of eyes in the street, offer
> Your making hands and your guts on skewers of pity.

Christian pity is one of the mistakes of our traditional anthropomorphic religion, says Stevens:

> The fault lies with an over-human god,
> Who by sympathy has made himself a man
> And is not to be distinguished when we cry
> Because we suffer [from] our oldest parent.
> . . . .
> If only he would not pity us so much,
> Weaken our fate, relieve us of woe both great
> And small, a constant fellow of destiny,
>
> A too, too human god, self-pity's kin
> And uncourageous genesis. . . . It seems
> As if the health of the world might be enough.

79

However dangerous a drug pity is, is it not unrealistic to envision men as everywhere healthy enough to dispense with it? If a too human God pitied us too much, does not the middle, limited location of humanity itself require its presence for the maintenance of a tolerable lot? Hardy made pity a celestial power. Hopkins, though he could reject even in his agony "carrion comfort," was not able in the end to live without a desperate dose of pity for his own suffering:

> My own heart let me have more pity on; let
> Me live to my sad self hereafter kind,
> Charitable; not live this tormented mind
> With this tormented mind tormenting yet . . .
> Come, poor Jack self, I do advise
> You, jaded, let be; call off thoughts awhile
> Elsewhere; leave comfort root-room. . . .

Perhaps one of the tasks of the moral philosopher is the re-evaluation and redefinition of compassion, in order that from him it may pass better understood into humane literature. Perhaps the poets have suffered so much that they have become not only active but hard. At any rate, if the present spirit of Caliban, romping riotously in poetry, excludes pity, then the element of earth is more hostile to humanity than the element of air, for Shakespeare made Ariel teach the revengeful Prospero to supplant revenge with humanity; Prospero said reflectively to Ariel:

> Hast thou, which art but air, a touch, a feeling
> Of their afflictions, and shall not myself,
> One of their kind, that relish all as sharply
> Passion as they, be kindlier moved than thou art?
> Though with their high wrongs, I am struck to the quick,

Yet with my nobler reason gainst my fury
Do I take part.

Here a poet praises the philosopher's instrument, reason, in that it restores a neglected value, compassion. Recent poets, however incoherent and ironical, have opened new experience to us through linguistic invention and have quickened and intensified the philosophical problem of doing and undergoing. Could we remind them, in return, of a fading quality in our common life, a slighted human excellence?

A

SPATIAL CONFIGURATION

IN

FIVE RECENT POETS

In a notable region of recent poetry three classes of spatial image stand out. These represent: (1) a point or line of division such as a crossroads or door; (2) a course or direction of motion such as a road, stairway, or path through the sky; (3) a place of consummation, such as a mountaintop, tower, or position in the heavens. A garden or "still center" also often represents consummation. These images are interspersed among the wide wealth of fresh images that masters of metaphors use; but the three named recur and join, for the reader, until they form a symbolic pattern. They seem to constitute a lightly sketched map of a section of what might be paradoxically called "moral space."

The first class of images includes doors, gates, junctions, and all types of intersection or division that symbolize moral crisis or the place of division between two kinds of life or sets of values. Sometimes walls containing windows or mirrors adumbrate such a boundary. Even a mask may be used to symbolize the distinction between moral appearance and reality. The first examples come from "The

Quest" series of sonnets by W. H. Auden. The third sonnet, "The Crossroads," is concerned with a railroad junction where friends are meeting and parting, "each to go to
his own mistake." The junction, says Auden, is like "all
quays and crossroads," for they are all places of decision
and farewell. Since this junction is encountered during
"the quest," the reader is expected to envisage behind the
overt description some branching of roads on the journey
in pursuit of the Holy Grail, therefore, a crisis in the religious life. The crossroads of the poem is own cousin to
the crossroads of the Hercules parable, rendered in picture
and story from the time of the Sophist Prodicus to the
virtuoso Shaftesbury and always pointing the distinction
between virtue and vice.

The first sonnet in the series is about a door. The door
represents the dramatic turning point in human life, the
separation of weal from woe, present security from possible
violent death, normal life from folly or fairyland.

> We pile our all against it when afraid
> And beat upon its panels when we die.

In the Epilogue the door image occurs again. In passing
over the threshold of a new day the soul is pictured as
beset with terrifying possibilities:

> . . . The rocks are big and bad,
> And death seems substantial in the thinning air;
>
> .   .   .   .
>
> . . . behind the doors of this ambitious day
> Stand shadows with enormous grudges, outside
> Its chartered ocean of perception
> Misshapen coast guards drunk with foreboding.

The door dividing sleeping from waking here collects into
its symbolism the shock of the self that has been nesting

for hours in its own informal world when suddenly con-
fronted with the hard public world; also the readjustment
required by a return "from a timeless world to a world
of time"; again the sudden realization of the menacing
attitude of this particular wartime world when the self
faces it anew; finally the general problem of the obligation
of an act of will and the sometimes conflicting obligation
to know enough to act wisely:

> . . . How can
> We will the knowledge that we must know to will?

Stephen Spender's poetry is full of the use of the door
or crossroads image. "Variations on My Life" begins:

> To knock and enter
> Knock and enter
> The cloudless posthumous door
> Where the slack guts are drawn into taut music.

The door is the line separating the poet's own present un-
fulfilled condition from the fruition of his aspiration.
What the door gives entrance to is

> The room white as paper
> With light falling on a white space
> Through high windows.

The meaning of this blessed room is, on the negative side,
release from pain, loneliness, and long journeys; on the
positive, universal acceptance of the facts of life and the
love of humanity. The act of choice is the determination
to exclude nothing from the hospitality of sympathy:

> . . . to ride on
> The whole quivering human machine!
>
> . . . .
>
> To explore all its gifts
> And nothing, nothing to refuse.

The same image that sets in motion "Variations on My Life" occurs in the middle of "Houses at Edge of Railway Lines," and the same meaning is implied. The poet wishes to leave the train he calls a "lurid shrieking cinder" and cross the threshold to the other and better world silently:

> . . . without knocking to enter
> The life that lies behind
> The edges of drawn blinds,
>
> . . . .
>
> Where love fills rooms, as gold
> Pours into a valid mould.

Windows cut the wall which separates fantasy from fact in "The Uncreating Chaos." The "summer-muscled" one, who feels but does not act, is commanded: "Alter your life." He is to note that

> . . . beyond windows of this waking dream
> Facts do their hundred miles an hour
> Snorting in circles round the plain.

The whole scheme of Day-Lewis's "The Magnetic Mountain" rests on the basis of the three types of image listed. The fourth part begins:

> Junction or terminus—here we alight.
> A myriad tracks converge on this moment.

The "myriad tracks" symbolize all the common habits and conventions that come to a full stop in the crisis of this war—this more-than-war—for the symbolism is again of a choice required of the young between safety, comfort, tradition on the one hand and the tragic venture for freedom and a better society on the other:

> . . . it's up to you, boys,
> Which shall it be? You must make your choice.

A Spatial Configuration in Five Recent Poets

> There's a war on, you know. Will you take your stand
> In obsolete forts or in no-man's land?

In T. S. Eliot's *Four Quartets* the image of an intersection occurs repeatedly. The intersection functions for
Eliot as junctions and doors do for the other poets cited—
as a place of "decision or farewell." It imposes the obligation of a moral choice, or signifies the terminus of one
world of values and the beginning of another. Throughout the volume Eliot is preoccupied with the sharp contrast between the world of time and eternity, the twitter-
ing world of common desire, sense experience, and human
weakness as set against the kingdom of peace and freedom.
The determination of the boundary line is a serious concern for the religious expert, he tells us in "Dry Salvages":

> . . . to apprehend
> The point of intersection of the timeless
> With time, is an occupation for the saint.

In "Little Gidding" the reader is addressed under the
person of any common traveler "taking any route, starting
from anywhere, at any time or any season" and bound for
the "world's end," that is, for arrival at the Ideal Com-
munion. The crossing of the common with the ideal way
is declared to be a place and time of religious purification:

> . . . You are here to kneel
> Where prayer has been valid . . .
> . . . the light fails . . .
> . . . in a secluded chapel . . .

The chapel in its turn is the universal place of meeting of
the human soul with its divine vocation:

> . . . the intersection of the timeless moment
> In England and nowhere.

89

The poet relates that he himself on his Everyman's pilgrimage "met one walking"—"a dead master . . . with brown baked features," and that the two walked on together "in concord at this intersection time of meeting nowhere." When implored to speak, the dead master, Dante's Brunetto, disclosed under the traditional veils of metaphor that progress beyond the intersection is possible only through the offices of "the refining fire." Here we observe the richness of meaning of the crossways. It is the confrontation of Everyman with the imperatives of the saint, the purgative process of prayer and ritual, the encounter with a character from the teacher and poet, Dante, and the passage, as suggested by him, through the spiritual testing place of Purgatory.

> The only hope. . . .
>> Lies in the choice of pyre or pyre—
>> To be redeemed from fire by fire.

The reference to an encounter with Brunetto at a crossroads, and the enlargement of this incident into its full significance against the background of *The Divine Comedy* remind us that embarkation upon a journey at a gateway or junction naturally leads to the process of the journey itself. Certainly in *The Four Quartets* there is concern with the religious pilgrimage in all its course, and the model of Dante's cosmic journey often shines through, as, for instance, in the lines reminiscent of the famous opening of the *Comedy:*

> In the middle, not only in the middle of the way
> But all the way, in a dark wood, in a bramble,
> On the edge of a grimpen, where is no secure foothold,
> And menaced by monsters. . . .

Dante's journey lies behind Eliot's poem, as the quest of

the Holy Grail lies behind Auden's sonnet sequence. Although the tone of Auden's "Quest" series is ultimately
serious, as the title suggests, it is shot through with sunny
secular humanism and irony. This is evident from Sonnet XIV, called "The Way." Here he satirizes those limited souls who imagine that they can pursue the moral
pilgrimage by following such superficial directions as are
found in encyclopedia articles or unexamined "tips."

The second class of image that we are concerned with
includes the courses and kinds of motion our poets envisage
as carrying one beyond a threshold or a crux. Such a
"way" is sometimes a stairway, a mountain slope, the track
of a dance, a bird, or a star. Often the traveler moves from
a position on the ground to a vantage point above it; or,
if the journey is a glorious one, the course may be through
the sky itself with bird or sun, or their emulator, the aviator. The progress may equally be from insignificant pe-
ripheral wandering, through the rising intensity of a
dance, to the ecstasy of a "still center" or the fruition of
an inclosed garden.

A typical progress is sketched by Stephen Spender in
the introductory song of *Ruins and Visions.* The poet's
beloved has been faithless to him, and he claims himself
justified in any terrible act of murder or suicide in revenge.
Then a second thought comes—a crisis is passed. He cele-
brates the arrival of the moral sublimation thus:

> . . . but supposing that I climb
>   Alone to a high room of clouds
> Up a ladder of the time
> And lie upon a bed alone
>   And tear a feather from a wing
> And listen to the world below

> And write round my high paper walls
> Anything and everything. . . .

Here the conquest of immediate crude feeling is figured as the climbing on a ladder into a room among the clouds. Spender often makes his course skyward for himself or his heroes. In one of his best known poems he represents the proud but doomed aviator as one who, having had commerce with hawk and eagle,

> paced the enormous cloud, almost had won
> War on the sun.

And in probably the best known of all his poems he makes the course of "the truly great" from beginning to end exalted among the stars:

> Near the snow, near the sun, in the highest fields
> See how these names are fêted by the waving grass
> And by the streamers of white cloud
> And whispers of wind in the listening sky. . . .
> Born of the sun they travelled a short while towards the sun
> And left the vivid air signed with their honor.

So full is Spender's poetry of lifted allusion to sky, sun, and cloud that the reader becomes convinced that for this poet all good journeys begin, end, and proceed there.

Yeats's orientation for his journeys is not so consistently lofty, but the meaning of the true course is not as different from Spender's as would at first appear. In his late groups of poems called "The Winding Stair" and "The Tower," he writes:

> I declare this tower is my symbol; I declare
> This winding gyring, spiring treadmill of a stair
> Is my ancestral stair.

The tower is falling into ruins like his decaying family,

his old man's body, and even like the nation and the time "half-dead at the top." Yeats clings to the dynamism of the upward climb and fights off the stasis of arrival and the dropping into decay.

> I summon to the winding ancient stair;
> Set all your mind upon the steep ascent;
> Upon the broken, crumbling battlement
> Upon the breathless starlit air,
> Upon the star that marks the hidden pole.

The climb up the old watchtower signifies for Yeats the passion and energy of warriors, lovers, saints, and workmen; the strength of magnanimity, laughter, and song; and the boldness that casts out remorse. Swift, Goldsmith, Burke, and Berkeley, whom he claims as his kinsmen, illustrated these characteristics; and they were all lovers of human liberty, champions of the weak, and bold idealists. As mounters of this "gyre" they hated

> A levelling, rancorous, rational sort of mind
> That never looked out of the eye of a saint
> Or out of drunkard's eye.

In one of his last poems, "An Acre of Grass," Yeats uses other symbols that intend the same notion of defiant energy, lust, and love, and convey this notion of images of ascent to high places: the piercing of clouds and the flight of the eagle:

> My temptation is quiet.
> . . . .
> Grant me an old man's frenzy,
> . . . .
> A mind Michael Angelo knew
> That can pierce the clouds,
> Or inspired by frenzy

Katharine Gilbert

Shake the dead in their shrouds;

. . . .

An old man's eagle mind.

We said that a course or direction of motion is often
symbolized by the rising intensity or rhythm of a dance
as well as by a mounting to high places. Yeats has a whole
group of poems on "Michael Robartes and the Dancer,"
and he uses the dance motive freely elsewhere. In dancing
as in climbing, his old man's eagle mind finds strong, wild
movement congenial: it is "the way" to consummation.
After describing the ecstatic improvised dancing of a
schizophrene "in desperate music wound," he says:

> that girl I declare
> A beautiful lofty thing.

In his stage directions for the dancing in "The Death of
Cuchalain" he demands a powerful, imperious type of
dancer who can move as in triumph or adoration. He says
he spits upon the meaningless delicacy of the ballet: "I
spit three times. I spit upon the dancers painted by Degas.
I spit upon their short bodices, their stiff stays, their toes
whereon they spin like peg-tops, above all upon that cham-
ber-maid face." And once more in the "Crazy Jane" series
Yeats makes old Jane extol the wild dance that speaks
"heart's truth" where "love is like the lion's tooth."

It is of the rhythmic circling of a round dance about a
"still center" that Eliot writes. In "East Coker" the rustic
turning round and round the fire is a token of concord
and of the regular recurrence of seasons and constellations.
But this regular beating and circling, while definitely
along the "way" toward consummation from such distracted and unmeaning motion as that of bits of paper

94

whirled in the wind or of fishing boats drifting, yet derives its value from the control at the center:

> At the still point of the turning world. Neither flesh nor
> fleshless;
> Neither from nor towards; at the still point, there the
> dance is.

The third class of images marks a place of consummation. As arrival must be functionally related to the setting-forth and the travel along a way, the statement of the meaning of consummation can be brief. The place often sought by our poets is either a height, connoting energetic poise, or a quiet center, connoting the fruition of ecstasy. The quarter chosen is often in the sky with eagles or falcons. Is this perhaps partly the influence of Gerard Manley Hopkins and his poem "The Windhover"? Probably the most concentrated use of the falcon image is in Day-Lewis's "Magnetic Mountain," where the poet seven times addresses Auden as a kestrel:

> . . . elate . . .
> My kestrel joy, O hoverer in wind,
>
> . . . .
>
> Chaired on shoulders of shouting wind.

"Chaste my kestrel"; "kestrel, my lucky star"; etc.

Hopkins himself not only likens the kestrel to Christ, but his favorite musician, Purcell, to a storm fowl, and man's mounting spirit to the "dare-gale sky-lark." In fact, so impressive is Hopkins's concern with birds and his fellow feeling for them that Robert Bridges, in giving his friend's poetry to the world, addressed him thus:

> Go forth: amidst our chaffinch flock display
> Thy plumage of far wonder, and heavenward flight.

At first glance there seems to be an incongruity in placing consummation both on high with suns and birds, on mountaintops and towers, and at the same time in the motionlessness of a center or the peace of a garden. What these two types have in common seems precisely to be the energy of ecstasy, the joy of consummation. Eliot warns against conceiving the still point of the turning world as static. Rather it is concentration: the complete realization of life and love. To use the Dantesque figures Eliot so often employs, it is the energy of the testing fire combined with the perfection of the mystic rose. The still charm, then, of a recalled rose garden of childhood suitably shadows forth for Eliot the divine spring of energy at the center of nature. The inclosure of the garden of love is again the image Auden has used to bring to completion his "Quest" sequence:

> Within these gates all opening begins:
> White shouts and flickers through its green and red,
>
> . . . .
>
> Here adolescence into number breaks
> The perfect circle time can draw on stone,
>
> . . . .
>
> All journeys die here; wish and weight are lifted.

Many more examples of the three types of imagery dealt with in this short study could be given. Further cases and elaboration would doubtless modify as well as fill out the argument. All that is suggested here is that (1) habitual preference for certain types of spatial image in the same period by a group of important poets is symptomatic of a common basic way of taking the world; (2) while the three types here handled now and then echo somewhat stereotyped images associated with specific doctrines, such as Jung's archetypism, Thomism, or Marxism, their use as a favored vehicle by poets of these varied and sometimes opposed persuasions argues a concern more universal than any of these doctrines; (3) in their combined drift they imply the tendency of these poets to engage their imagination with a serious moral, humanistic, or religious attitude toward life.

RECENT CATHOLIC VIEWS

ON

ART AND POETRY

ALL POETRY is divided into two parts: the coming into being and the shaping up. Those concerned with poetry have realized this at least ever since Socrates, commanded in a dream to make poetry, worried because—though he could fit words musically together—he could not invent. Trying to clear his duties during his last days in prison, he "composed"; but he had to borrow the original substance from Aesop, being himself sterile. Recently Catholic writers, artists, and lovers of art have poured a new intensity into the meaning of these two parts of all art and their mutual adjustment. The freshness of their views comes from the thoroughness with which, reviving old thoughts and observing new agonies, they have made the "coming into being" into travail and birth out of a "dark night," the "shaping up" into rightly ruled construction in any material; and the final fusion of the two is negotiable only by Divinity. The most dramatic assertion of the constructive half of art is Eric Gill's: "I say that to make a drainpipe is as much the work of an artist as it is to make paintings or poems."[1] "Artists belong in the class of all workmen, doing useful jobs." The second part, the mystical birth of poetry, is best described by Jacques Maritain: "In a way, . . . [the artist] is not of this world, being, from the moment he begins working for beauty, on the road which leads upright souls to God and makes invisible things clear to them by visible."[2] Neo-Catholic theorists of the artistic process might display an emblem to picture their paradox: a drawing of Christ as the divine carpenter. The suggestion receives support from a sentence in *Art and Scholasticism:* "Pondering the art or activity peculiar to the *artifex,* . . . [the Doctors of the Middle Ages] pondered the activity which Our Lord chose to exercise throughout His hidden life; they pondered also, in a way, the activity even of the Father; for they knew that the virtue of art is to be predicated peculiarly of God, like Goodness and Justice, and that the Son, plying His poor man's trade, was still the image of the Father and of His action."[3]

Let us follow the Catholic breaking down of the two crucial concepts, "craft" and "inspiration," into elements, and examine the nature of that final element which is used to bring them together.

As craftsman, an artist is a human being especially impelled to work himself outward. In contrast with the thinker, whose habit is introspective, the artist belongs with practical men, who deal with things, and whose attention is directed to the environment. In the insistence that art, by nature, makes a work, a work that stands by itself outside the workman, the Neo-Catholic accents his typical realism. Modern aestheticians, it is asserted, "penetrated with subjectivism and the doctrine of empathy,"[4] have missed the essential feature in the creative operation of artists. At the base of all authentic explanation of the artistic act is placed its *pure objectivity.* The literal meaning of the word "objective" is emphasized: *ob-jective* equals "thrown over against"—*jeté dans l'être.* In the background of these phrases of the Neo-Thomists is Book VI of the *Nicomachean Ethics* where the line is drawn between the artistic virtue and intelligence of man and his moral character or prudence. "Art . . . has its excellence [or perfect development] in something other than itself, but this is not so with prudence." Prudence fulfils itself in the good of the agent. In St. Thomas this becomes: "Making is an action passing into outward matter whereas doing is an action abiding in the agent." The free gloss of Maritain on the Thomistic definition of such "making," "*poiein,*" "*poéticité*" is as follows:

Art as such has for its end, not to know, but to produce or create,—not in the mode of nature, as radium produces helium, nor as one living being engenders another, but in the mode of spirit and freedom. . . . [Art] is concerned with the productivity of the intelligence *ad extra.* . . . Because of . . . [intelligence's] superabundance it has an intrinsic tendency to express and manifest itself in the world [*au dehors*], to sing.[5]

This native propulsion or need of speech must, in the next place, submit itself to training in order to become art. So St. Thomas makes art not an ephemeral adjective of a human being, but a persisting habit. The native propensity becomes a fund of energy and expertness always at the owner's disposal. In the days when art was actually identified with craft, the apprentice learned his trade in a workshop or studio, and "copied line upon line the very living and varied action of his master." There was thus built into the youthful organism a skill that could be relied upon to furnish through the years well-made objects for human use. But as the master adapted his habit to the shape of the event, so also the pupil learned to do. The life and mobility of the skill was presumed to pass into the apprentice along with the fixed outlines of the tradition. In this sense art as craft was action upon matter as free as disciplined. Maritain calls the artist's habits living rules.

The last element named in our analytical process, viz., the freely swinging pointer of the craftsman's habit, inevitably limits the number of craftsmen. But on the whole, wherever there is working reason employed in shaping matter to useful ends, there is, in the view before us, the artist. In other words, the definition of craftsman, in the main, concerns only broad human traits: the will to produce, submission to discipline, and the possession of the right rule in the mind. The specifications do not call for rare gifts or extraordinary powers. The making of shoes, ships, and painted pictures alike becomes art, differentiated only by the distinctions of material and place of future service: In a word, art is continuous with all trades and skills.

Eric Gill's whole autobiography might be called a free commentary on the Neo-Scholastic conception of the artist's process. Cutting letters in tombstones was his special craft. He turned to this when he became disgusted with his place as a young architect's draughtsman for the Ecclesiastical Commission in London, and sought elsewhere an honest job and a true art. What made him rebellious in the architect's office was the perception of lack of integrity in the business that went forward. There the workman was not in the work. The practice of drawing went on in utter independence of, and even with ridicule of, what the drawing was for. The draughtsmen made "twiddles on paper," and the workmen somewhere else were supposed to turn the twiddles into lively, sculptured ornament, he complained. The end or rule was out of joint with the means or manufacture. The ecclesiastical intention was that the drawing should realize itself in stone for the glory of God according to the Anglican confession. But the draughtsmen never touched stone and they were agnostic. Gill said that he wished to "be a workman and demand a workman's rights, the right to design what he made; and a workman's duties, the duty to make what he designed."[8] All the canons of Thomist doctrine he believed to be satisfied by the art of carving letters as he intended to follow it: a right form coming directly from a right rule in the mind; no imitation, no sprawling emotion; a thing made, not the image of a thing; the "making" conducted according to the controlling conditions and regulations of a "trade," the production of an obvious utility. These are his words:

Lettering has this . . . advantage over other arts; at its very base, conjoined and inseparable, are the fair and the fit—most obviously useful and depending for its beauty upon nothing but man's musical sense. The shapes of letters do not derive their beauty from any sensual or sentimental reminiscence. No one can say that the O's roundness appeals to us only because it is like that of an apple or of a girl's breast or of the full moon. We like the circle because such liking is connatural to the human mind. And no one can say lettering is not a useful trade by which you can honestly serve your fellow men and earn an honest living. Of what other trade or art are these things so palpably true? Moreover it is a precise art. You don't draw an A and then stand back and say: there, that gives you a good idea of an A as seen through an autumn mist, or: that's not a real A but gives you a good effect of one. Letters are things, not pictures of things.[7]

In accenting the *homo artifex*, i.e., the artist as good workman and shaper, the Neo-Catholics have gone as far as possible into precedents, and, some might feel, into speculative regions. For the skilled maker, in his religious orientation, acknowledges descent from God, the prime Maker and Builder. The infinite God, to be sure, makes all things by the simple effluence of His Wisdom. His light rays out, giving form and being to all creatures, just as physical light gives visible boundaries and spatial relatedness to the common objects of natural vision. Of course, in this sense, man cannot make. But even so, the craftsman fashions his habit on the habit of Deity.

Having pursued the analysis of art as craft to its religious fruition, let us follow the Catholic analysis of art as inspiration.

The first condition of poetizing, says Maritain, is the interior silence. There is a recoil from the senses upon the center of the self and a long germinating slumber. The poet's retreat to the interior of his soul is as natural, he tells us, as the return of the bird to its nest. And when the soul returns to its center, it carries with it to "the mysterious nest of the soul" the whole world which it has put in fee.

How has it put the whole world in fee? By collecting much experience and then hoarding it. His collection of much experience is the result in the first instance of the poet's peculiar capacity for suffering, not merely "suffering" in the sense of "feeling pain," but in the sense of suffering things. To "suffer" things, to receive their signature, is a relationship to the environment more emotional and intimate than knowing, more speculative and removed than loving. That it is the latter precludes absolute consummation in mysticism, which implies complete absorption in the object. The "suffering" of the poet is a special synthesis of affection and vision, but distinct from either alone. The verbs used by Maritain mean "take," "seize," or "capture," and the process becomes reciprocal. The sight or sound that "takes" the soul becomes in its turn captive. The artist "suffers" the impact of the active energies of things only in his turn to "embowel" them.

The Neo-Catholic alters and elaborates artistic impressionability almost beyond recognition, for he relates it not to the semblance or appearance but to the actual Presence or true meaning. The suffering involved in the poetic emotion, Maritain says, follows from the poet's kinship with the very secret of the concrete, the inwardness of essences, the *"quiddités, qualités, talités, haecceités, ipseités"* with which single and real existences teem. The poet has a voracious appetite for Being, and Being as such. Marcel de Corte describes the poet's penetration of Being thus: "There is something really existent which poetical experience seizes and ravishes mysteriously."[8] Thus, we see, it is not the mere senseless flux—the world's foolish weather, so to speak—that the poet suffers, but rather

Meaning motion fans fresh [his] wits with wonder.

He captures the formative actions of things that he, with his peculiarly formative capacities, inclines to. He grasps a thing's intention or direction, its number, weight, proportion, analogy. His own tense individuality and realized energy make him more than any other human being "infinitely aware" of the "typical existent" in its full flowering or at its being's crown.

The sensitiveness of the artist, then, means in the view now before us that the life and energy in man meets and assimilates the life and energy in things.

The phase of collection is followed by the phase of recollection. Or to be more accurate, the phase of harvesting impressions is followed by the phase of their storage in the phantasy and memory. Memory's title, Mnemosyne, mother of the Muses, implies the transition of potential poetry from an external place and relation to the poet's mood to an interior residence. It signifies the conversion of sense impact, culled events, into spiritual substance. Memory gives the Muse a thesaurus of forms.

What the inspired artist has turned in this way into coin of spirit, and memorized or "learned by heart," he holds long in reserve and cherishes as a rich fund of individual shapes and impressions. This hoarding temperament is in sharp contrast to the normal way of the practical man who spends experience as fast as he gets it. The life of the man of affairs goes forward in a process of quick exchange with the environment. He does not mull over the impressions that he receives, but passes them out again to the busy human congregation in which he spends his time, much in the form in which he receives them. The result is that the normal practical man is almost always in play at his surface, and at different points of his surface. He is distracted in the sense that his occupation calls for lively adaptation to varied external demands. T. S. Eliot reminds us of the strained, time-ridden faces

> Filled with fancies and empty of meaning
> Tumid apathy with no concentration
> Men and bits of paper. . . .[9]

The poet, on the other hand, is ill adjusted to surface calls, because his life is within. His major function is, so to speak, to sleep. Only he must be a good dreamer. Indeed, the words "slumber," "retreat," "ingathering" spell inactivity only from the point of view of the comparatively insignificant conscious activity we are most used to. The soul in retreat has its own kind of peculiar intense activity. "In poesy man is concentered at the base of his human reality. There he yields to quietude—but not in the least to the illusory quietude of the inactivity and vacancy of thought, but to this infinite quietude in which all the energies and all the relations are in activity."[10]

What, then, is the intense activity of the recoil? The collected and stored energies continue to operate when they are in the poet's mind. They engage, there, with the general psychic power. The psyche as a whole swells within the wider Spirit that moves through all things. In this way the Inspiration of the poet reveals its identity with the Prime Craftsman, the Architect of the World.

What has happened, indeed, is convergence from different directions upon a paradigm of Creativity. A maker of ships or shoes models his craft, however much he molds matter and coalesces with the "practical man," in the last resort on Pure Essence or Productive Intelligence. A singer of lyrics feels the stirrings and pressure of this same Productive Intelligence far within his spiritual bowels. The ideas that seem so far apart—methodical skill and ecstatic imagining—come together because both involve engendering and direction by the same Being. This common spring and law makes them commensurable, and the craftsman, however humble, weaves an analogue of poetry in his coat, and the poet, however bubbling and inflamed, abides by the lines and rules of technique.

Anyone who follows this theory sympathetically must be impressed by its aesthetic insight, moral sensitiveness, and dialectical subtlety. But difficulties remain. The two conceptions seem to get together partly because they are themselves ambiguous, and partly because they are subsumed under a vague all-mothering Idea. This vague concept is that of Pure Act or Being Itself, which grounds both craft and the "factive idea," or inspiration, of the poet. In part, Being is treated as the "luxury" or "aboundingness" of whatever is, i.e., analogical Being. One might even go for light on this Catholic concept to Santayana's gloss on Spinozistic Substance: "the realm of essence in its omnimodal immensity—in its capacity for infinite variation of forms." Or one might think of Goethe's observation on the elements in Being that nourish genius: "All is influence except ourselves." Cocteau himself in "Professional Secrets" says: "The poet is a believer. In what? In everything." M. Maritain's drift at times seems this way, for example, when he is discussing the theory of poetry of M. de Corte. De Corte insists that poetry has nothing to do with the conceptual understanding, but bears directly on pure Being. Yes, replies Maritain, always remembering that Being, as the poet's intuition grasps it and is moved by it, is infinitely varied, generous, and rich. The Being which the poet cognizes, and which burns and lives and springs in him, is the heart of all that is intimate and the delicacy of all that is fragile. The reality of Being must not be confused with a naked abstraction.

However, interfering with this concept of Being, infinitely wide, deep, and colorful, is the concept of the God-man. The artist's productive soul then becomes the theater of a moral combat, and a good and wise analogue of himself is seen at war with a Devil, who is, in a quasi-human fashion, bad and foolish. Or if these two major protagonists are not stirring the poet's depths, angels, black and white, are. This is, of course, picture-thinking, the approach by myth to the reasons for things.

A complex theory, such as the present one, may well display a paradoxical emblem that brings together in a pictorial metaphor a carpenter and God. But a flickering concept that unites and separates pure Being and an anthropomorphic God is hardly a stable basis for a philosophy of poetry.

NOTES

1. *Art* (London, 1935), p. 4.
2. *Art and Scholasticism* (New York, 1930), p. 38.
3. *Ibid.,* pp. 20-21.
4. Marcel de Corte, *Revue Thomiste,* XLII (1937), 392.
5. Jacques Maritain, *Situation de la poésie* (Paris, 1938), pp. 96-97.
6. *Autobiography* (London, 1940), p. 115.
7. *Ibid.,* p. 120.
8. De Corte, *op. cit.,* p. 368.
9. *Collected Poems, 1909-1935* (New York, 1936), p. 217.
10. Raïssa Maritain, "Sens et non-sens en poésie," in Jacques Maritain, *Situation de la poésie,* p. 46 n.

THE RELATION BETWEEN

AESTHETICS

AND ART-CRITICISM

IT HAS BEEN peculiarly difficult to avoid the too much and the too little in distinguishing the art-critic from the philosopher of art. Loose thought has lumped them together as intellectually concerned with art. Precise thought and jealousy for the cultural compartment have erected high barriers between them. Our chief historian of literary criticism had an unerring scent for the metaphysical taint in criticism, and by the very thoroughness of his exclusion of aesthetic seemed to verge on making, on his own part, a metaphysical pronouncement. Morelli in the last century became the father of a school in the criticism of painting that repudiated before all else "any bump of philosophy." Wilenski has recently taken a firm step forward in this same partitioning tradition by proposing that any overstepping of boundaries in the various concerns with art shall automatically mean forfeiture of a degree for a candidate in a specific subject.[1] Aesthetics has not failed to reciprocate these amenities. For Croce the first business of an aesthetician is to determine the concept "art," and that determination rests upon a speculative and ideal history of spirit. Franz Böhm, speaking from the point of view of the Heidelberg school, cleaves sharply the empirical concern with the facts of art and the derivation of style concepts from the philosophical deduction of the "value-moment," questions of fact from questions of worth.[2] Grudin insists that aesthetics is a form of logic, that it manipulates verbal symbols, and that any other concern with art in respect to it assumes the role of datum.[3]

Whatever one thinks ultimately about the relation of art-criticism and aesthetics, one must agree with the incisive captains of the two camps that alliances, blendings, and compromises ought to follow and not precede the best possible discrimination of territory and aim. What, then, should be the preliminary statement of the distinction of function between these two disciplines? The critic aims to *sharpen an image;* the philosopher to *define a sphere.*

In sharpening the image a critic tries to set in relief both the detail and the gross contour of the work. Just as improved methods of making and adjusting lantern slides have made possible increased visibility of the images on the screen, so the devices of the good critic intensify for the beholder both the sensuous qualities, the intellectual "bonds and tyes," and the individual physiognomy of the whole. From Dionysius of Halicarnassus to Lascelles Abercrombie critics have isolated the simplest elements of verbal music and of spoken rhythm in order to make manifest the contribution of these musical atoms to the final poetical effect. We are aware of "tactile values" in Giotto and Masaccio as we were not before Berenson pointed them out. The symbolism of Dürer's *Melencolia I* has been richly documented for us by Panofsky so that we respond to the image as a whole with new eyes. Ruskin taught his own generation to notice the light values in Turner and the connotation of Milton's words. Today we are made aware of the feeling value of the thirds and sixths in Brahms's waltzes, the "poignant, lacerating ninths" in Wolf's songs by Ernest Newman; the *Helligkeit* of organ tones by J. Biehle. Whether the critic lingers longest with the isolable qualities, with the logical intervals and relations, or with the total "habit," his aim throughout is to impress upon us more vividly the stamp of the image's form.

This definition of a critic holds, whatever the disagreements within the profession about the number of planes in a work of art. Whether the poem "refers to" or "reveals" a reality outside itself or not, whether there is or is not a layer that has conceptual significance underneath the layers composing the decorative schema, there is always at least the artistic essence that lies within the frame. This essence the uninstructed always need to be taught to contemplate more penetratingly. It is not only the great traditional critics, for example, Winckelmann and Lessing, that have given us new aesthetic organs. Any successful critic to the degree that he is successful adds to the sensitivity of our responding mechanism. The end of the critic, says Mr. T. S. Eliot, is simply to enable us to perceive; that is, to return to the work of art with improved perception and with intensified, because more conscious, enjoyment.[4] M. Mauron says in almost the same words that the critic's aim is to heighten our pleasure by clarifying our consciousness; Ernest Newman, that it is to intensify our experience. This conception is not new. Even certain good Victorian critics with a moralistic bias said after all much the same thing. For Matthew Arnold the end of criticism is to see the object as in itself it really is; for Ruskin, to induce energy of contemplation. The sum of the sayings is that criticism works to illuminate the matter in hand and to lighten the beholder's darkness so that the picture or poem before him shines into his consciousness as an intelligible and shapely individuality.

But this unanimity of opinion regarding the perfect critic presupposes something. It presupposes that there is an object there; that it has shape and unity; that it has matter that is logical and fitted to intellectual illumination. Suppose when the critic enters into the alleged "object" in order to stamp it out more clearly, it refuses to be one. Suppose the firm contour, the logical texture, the definite qualities will not answer to the critical summons. Conceivably that upon which the critic feels moved to operate sympathetically may not be altogether an *object*, a one.

Perhaps the expression "a one" may frighten the reader, as if Plotinus were approaching. The critic, we say with that reader, ought not to approach the work of art with preconceived ideas of what the work of art ought to be. It is his business to let the work operate on him and tell him—he lying wisely passive—what it is. But that the work should be a one would seem to be such an elementary condition of his ability to function that he is scarcely conscious of it. For, suppose that the matter before him tells him conflicting stories that will not be reconciled even in his wisely passive head. Suppose part of it does not speak at all, but is dumb or drones. Is it, or is it not, his function to report this unsuccess in bringing alive to his own consciousness the logic and the individuality of the piece before him? Presumably no one would insist that every alleged art object to which the critic exposes his sensitive plate has actually "come through."

Reflection on these possibilities shows us that the work of the critic can hardly be summed up as simply aiding the perception of what is given. He has corrective as well as contemplative offices. Even from Aristotle himself, the perfect critic according to Mr. Eliot, derives the canon which enables critics to mend what is wrong as well as see what is right. Aristotle said that a good tragedy must be in such a sense one that the addition or withdrawal or alteration of any part would spoil the whole. The reference to these irreconcilable parts that are excrescences or deficiencies or misplacements implies that the critic is aware of alleged cases of art that cannot be perceived as single objects. In such a case his business is not to be wisely passive, but to be wisely active. A musical critic has suggested that this part of the critic's work is ideally compared to plastic surgery. The critic can say of the finished product

. . . where it is clumsily worked, where it is muddled, where it fails in that steady procession from premises to conclusion that all good art ought to show. . . . [He] might have told Bach that now and then his piano works were not so much finished as merely terminated . . . ; Beethoven or Brahms when he was becoming too mechanical, too text-bookish, in his 'working-out'—in that always awkward moment, for example, of transition from the exposition section to the development section . . . ; Wagner that he was weakening a passage by gross excess of sequential repetition . . . ; Debussy when the whole-tone scale had exhausted its welcome . . . ; this English composer that piety was a poor substitute for inspiration, even in the British oratorio; another, that he was in danger of exploiting to death a certain sequence of descending chromatic harmonies; another that a certain sort of bogus polyphony was beginning to reveal all too plainly its complete absence of a secret.[5]

This indication of needed aesthetic surgery presupposes that the critic may be baffled in his effort to see and set in relief a long series of ones. Without any arrogance of a priori ideals, the course of his beholding may run other than smoothly. On the basis of what, then, does the passive labor cease and the active labor come in? "Out of the fund of a richer experience of art,"[6] we are told. If this be true, the critic beholds his alleged object not with a nice one-to-one correspondence, but with a mind constituted for the time being by the energies incorporated in it from many experienced objects. The thing is looked at by the hardly acknowledged light of almost innumerable examples that have distilled into essence of critical mind. And in this sense the critic measures his object by something external to the object. In so doing, he does not stretch it on a Procrustean bed, but—so we must allow him—still measures it by a standard relevant, and on a properly liberal interpretation, immanent. He measures it by what he conceives the thing itself wants to be but has failed to be.

This wider something that measures artistic success and that sometimes artificially produces artistic unity by surgery; this regulative principle that both stays inside the object and travels freely beyond it, is the critic's matured sense of *kind*. In building up his sense of *kind* the critic develops what the old psychologists used to call "wit."

Wit characteristically seeks out the similarities and associations between things, whereas judgment characteristically seeks out the differences and unlikenesses between things. The critic with his strong native wit, then, passes constantly and sensitively from poem to poem, fugue to fugue, picture to picture, building up a sense of a style. This sense of style is at once an awareness of the defining marks and relations in kindred works and an operating norm in respect to them.

Now philosophers of art also deal with *kinds*. But with them, the sense of kind is primary and at the focus of attention rather than a half-acknowledged organ dimly felt to be functioning. As the philosophical temperament is on the whole rather discriminative than associative, the aesthetician from the very beginnings of his experiencing of art objects lingers by preference on the borderline between art and nonart. He often takes over what generations of critics have pronounced good and have set in relief as good and tries to match the nature of this as a whole with some adequate definition, a definition that both tells what it is and what it is not. Our philosopher savors, then, preferentially the special quality of what is within the contour of a product as over against the special quality of what is outside. And when he lingers within the art object he gravitates toward the place of problematic interpretation. He likes to stay by the swaying barrier between matter shaped and matter recalcitrant. Since his forte is judgment rather than wit, he tends to take over the volume of others' labor as a whole, to perceive it as a qualified totality, and to make intelligible to himself and others, the series or system of qualified totalities. Thus will he get a maximum sense of precise differentiation. He builds up not a sense of style, but of the universe of discourses; he distinguishes spheres.

The whole history of aesthetics illustrates this interpretation of the aesthetician. For example, Plato defended the thesis that poetry is not theology, and that Homer is not a military manual but imagery; Aristotle asserted that poetry is not history; Bruno that it is not the application of rules; Kant that what taste approves is not logical, yet, again, not dissimilar to logic. The philosopher of art is interested primarily not quite in the place where two roads meet, but in the area where two fields have a tendency to overlap. He would distinguish the sphere of practical persuasion from that of the ranging fancy; the sphere of the recipe from that of plastic creation; the sphere of philosophical theory from that of unattached form; the sphere of profitable lesson from that of nontendential emotional fulfilment. That rich fund of experience upon the basis of which the philosopher of art "places" a phenomenon is experience in the refining attributes of the major fields of human interest. When a literary critic would surgically cleanse Galsworthy or George Eliot of the moral fallacy, he might well take counsel of the philosopher who knows by profession the differentiating property of morality. His life is spent in tracing and sorting universals.

Since the art-critic, however modestly he holds himself to his primary business of seeing the object for what it really is, cannot do even this without comparing and relating the given with the many kindred objects that make up his sense of style and his empirical norm; and since the philosopher of art cannot define a sphere nor identify with sure tact the nature of a universal, without having apprehended it innumerable times in the concrete, we are driven in the end, I think, to consider these two functions, however distinguishable, as abstractions from a total ideal concern with art. The philosopher should be the critic's expert consultant on the precise meaning of the predicate terms "art," "beautiful," "ugly," "moral," "religious," "end," "means," "matter," "form," etc. In adjusting his definition exactly to the proposed sphere, the philosopher needs the constant aid of the richer experience and finer analysis of detail of the critic. If the needy critic or philosopher can find the required brother laborer within his own organism, the more speedily and amicably is the total task completed.

The union of the two functions within one personal substance is not so unrealizable an ideal as one is at first prone to think. Mr. T. S. Eliot has recently crowned Aristotle as the ideal critic. But I suppose Aristotle did not cease to be a philosopher at the coronation. Mr. Eliot says that Aristotle does not treat of any critical matter in poetry which he does not illuminate. But all the special points in poetry which he illuminates are illuminated largely because they are bathed in the light of logical and metaphysical distinctions worked out patiently elsewhere in the Aristotelian corpus: the four causes; potentiality and actuality; telescoping forms; the relation of pleasure to action. I would venture the assertion that no more satisfactory basis for criticism could be found than some variant of Aristotle's metaphysics. It is such a framework that gives support and cogency to Santayana's essay on the nature of poetry and Lascelles Abercrombie's theory of poetry; and these discourses seem to me successful both as criticism and as philosophy. Of Coleridge's rank as a critic no encomium is ever needed; and A. C. Bradley has on occasion been rated even higher. If A. C. Bradley competes with Coleridge, it is no less true that his criticism stands firmly fixed in Hegel as Coleridge's did in Kant. No more distinguished critic of Italian Renaissance painting is active today than Sig. Lionello Venturi, and he writes: "It is obvious, then, that a critical history of art should benefit from aesthetics as well as from historical facts."[7]

My conclusion is that it is the function of criticism, *qua* abstract ideal method, to sharpen the image; of the philosophy of art, *qua* ideal abstract method, to define spheres; but that the ideal trafficker with art is like Diotima's δαίμων who "conveys and takes across" the definitions of universals to the critics, and the clarified images and norms of the critic to the philosopher, and so "spans the chasm which divides them."

NOTES

1. "The Organization of the Study of Art History," *Deuxième Congrès International d'Esthétique et de Science de l'Art*, II, 73-76.

2. *Die Logik der Asthetik* (Tübingen, 1930), p. 57.

3. *A Primer of Æsthetics* (New York, 1930), p. 241.

4. *The Sacred Wood* (New York, 1930), pp. 11-15.

5. Ernest Newman, "On Musical Surgery," *A Musical Motley* (New York, 1925), pp. 96, 97.

6. *Ibid.*

7. *History of Art Criticism* (New York, 1936), p. 29.

ART:

REMINDER AND DELIGHT

"ART: REMINDER AND DELIGHT"
IS A REVIEW OF ANANDA K. COOMARASWAMY'S
"WHY EXHIBIT WORKS OF ART?" AND
"FIGURES OF SPEECH OR FIGURES OF THOUGHT"

THESE TWO BOOKS are a first and second series of essays, lectures, book reviews, and broadcasts dealing in rich and varied fashion with aspects of the philosophy of art which the author himself calls "traditional or normal" but to which he gave an individual stamp in his lifetime of erudite writing. In the sense of the word which he wished to reinstate he "ornamented" the tradition; i.e., he filled out its meaning and strengthened its effectiveness by supplying further equipment (*Figures,* pp. 87-97). No one else living among us was able so to interweave the languages and cultural perspectives of Sanskrit, Greek, medieval Scholastic, American Indian, and modern Western European, to this end. The ornamental treatment does not result in the presentation of any contrasting schemes of ideas or sets of postulates. There is here hardly a comparative aesthetics. Rather, as Mr. Coomaraswamy himself says in the Preface to *Figures of Speech or Figures of Thought,* "The subject matter of the whole is consistently one and the same, and no other than that of my *Why Exhibit Works of Art"* (p. 5). It is wholly justifiable therefore to summarize the main sense of the two books in a series of succinct statements. The doctrine is as follows:

1. The first excellence of art is its truth or "iconographical correctness," i.e. its appropriate rendering in visible terms of central religious teaching. Art is one kind of metaphysical statement, and artists and true connoisseurs are serious students of final things.

2. An excellence of art, hardly second to the first because so closely involved with it, is its moral instructiveness. Art is a guide to right action. It is good in so far as it conduces to a happy and useful life.

3. Artists are not first of all beings with a special sensitivity, vision, or plastic power, but with a "vocation," i.e. a call to give religious instruction through graphic means. In the larger sense all men are artists who make things in the spirit of a vocation.

4. Art has a right to freedom, not from the censorship of those responsible for the community's well-being, but from commercial pressures and pulls. Art is bound and free as religion is bound and free.

5. The beauty of art is to remind rather than to delight. Aesthetic savor fulfils its function when it becomes a support for contemplation. For example, the "aesthetic shock" of the loveliness of the dewdrop passes properly into an awareness of the transitoriness of all living things (*Figures,* pp. 200-211).

6. Just as there is only a minor distinction of accent in art's truth as spoken by the spatially separated Oriental, Thomist, and American Indian, so the history of styles in its temporal succession yields only accidental variations. Truth is eternal, not progressive or conditioned, and art

being the symbolic communication of truth, is also essentially identical from age to age.

7. The current emphasis on aesthetic surface, on formal elements in abstraction from "literary" meaning, and on "function" without consideration of religious symbolism, is provincial—"bourgeoisie fantasy" (*Why Exhibit,* p. 95).

We are in debt to Mr. Coomaraswamy for the vigor and unique form in which certain important ideas are here set out, e.g.: that the referents of symbolic art are of consequence for the habit of the work as a whole; that the function of art engages with other life-functions and with what philosophy envisages; that aspects of contemporary aesthetics are conditioned and naïve. But even though he has emphasized what many neglect, he has neglected or even denied what many with justice perceive. It is unfortunate that in fighting narrowness he has himself at times been narrow. Indeed much of the value of these essays seems to lie in the rich and vivid aesthetic surface the author, almost in spite of himself, has been able to give to the familiar doctrine of Plotinus and St. Augustine. For example, "Samvega, 'Aesthetic Shock,'" (chap. xii, *Figures*) certainly has much in common with the "delicious troubling" of the soul in ecstasy as described by Plotinus. But to know how Buddhists handle the concept and to acquire the metaphor of the horse struck by a whip for aesthetic shock is agreeable learning.

Since, as we have noted, the doctrine here promulgated is repeated in different forms, and limited in extent, its validity may be examined illustratively in a single context. The gist of the title article "Why Exhibit Works of Art?" is as follows: An art museum exists "to take care of ancient or unique works of art which are no longer in their orig-

inal places or no longer used as was originally intended"
(p. 7). The museum has no direct obligation to living
artists. Furthermore, the exhibiting of the ancient and
unique works is not a primary function. However, if the
art treasures are exhibited, it must be for the purpose of
educating the visitors, i.e. by giving them instruction in
the original intention of the works and in pointing out
how the composition is adapted to the conveyance of metaphysical truth. "The Museum exhibition should amount
to an exhortation to return to . . . savage levels of culture"
(p. 13), in the sense that art on savage levels was made by
expert craftsmen and was fitted into the theory of a whole
life. "If we are to offer an education in agreement with
the innermost nature and eloquence of the exhibits themselves . . . this will not be an education in sensibility, but
an education in philosophy, in Plato's and Aristotle's sense
of the word, for whom it means ontology and theology and
the map of life, and a wisdom to be applied to everyday
matters" (p. 20).

Let the examination begin with the phrase: "not an
education in sensibility." One may believe that the author
means: "not an education in sensibility only." Often such
a qualification is made. But often also this champion of
ontology opposes education of the senses, feelings, and emotions through discipline in the arts. Surely, however, this
is to omit one of the primary opportunities and blessings
of art. In a sophistic passage (p. 20) Mr. Coomaraswamy
suggests that to teach men to feel is (1) to teach them
what they already know because they are not "hard-hearted
animal[s]," and (2) to make the materials of education
"spectacular," "personal," "anecdotal," or "flatter[ing]."
But it was Mr. Coomaraswamy's own favored Plato who

taught that the end of education is to learn to feel rightly, i.e., to have pleasures and pains in the right objects and in the right way. Refinement and sharpening of the senses and emotions is at least as much needed as iconology. It is needed in itself, and for the sake of that very "whole or holy man" that is Mr. Coomaraswamy's ideal (p. 81).

Next let us note Mr. Coomaraswamy's position that if a museum exhibits its treasures it does so by grace and not by primary vocation. Here again there is a false opposing of two interdependent functions: caring for and enjoying the use of. It is at least as frivolous to save for saving's sake as to rejoice the eyes without understanding the original intention of a picture. It is surely contrary to any ideal of "wholeness" to be intrusted with things of extraordinary value and efficacy and not to let their light shine.

Mr. Coomaraswamy says the museum has no obligation to living artists, and that exhibition of their works amounts to giving them free advertising. Their only grounds, he says, for wishing to be "hung" would be vanity or need—presumably, financial need. Would not a fairer judgment be that the best among them have something to say which is a little ahead of common apprehension or in a special idiom so that the meditation of a patient and intelligent explicator is indicated? In interpreting and presenting to the public Turner and Marin, neither Ruskin nor Stieglitz thought his artist merely vain or needy. The interpreters found a fresh and important vision deserving to be shared.

Mr. Coomaraswamy's bête noire is aesthetics. Since he fixes the meaning of the term by its etymology, and does not believe in progress, it would seem futile, for one who believes in the history of aesthetics as precisely the progressive enrichment of understanding in matters relating to art, to argue with him. He thinks of Pater and Valéry as typical exponents of aesthetics. Unquestionably their refining analysis of the sensuous surface of art belongs to the aesthetician's field. But there also belongs to it a rich literature dealing with art's symbolism stemming from Ernst Cassirer's notable volumes on *Symbolic Forms,* and including now the whole wealth of the Warburg Institute's output; also such subtle analyses of musical symbolism as may be found in the writings of Susanne Langer and Kathi Meyer. Again, exact definition of critical terms used with respect to art has been a primary concern of most recent writers in the field, as witness C. J. Ducasse's discrimination of art, beauty, ugliness; Theodore Greene's and John Hospers's examination of meaning and truth as related to the arts, and R. G. Collingwood's study of the place and function of the imagination. Art's moral effects and obligations are also the subject of many recent studies such as Herbert Read's *Art and Society* and D. W. Gotshalk's *Art and the Social Order.* The answers are not all in traditional terms and therefore would not be acceptable to Mr. Coomaraswamy, but the authors are aware of the traditional problems, and the answers differ only because the authors think more is now to be taken into account than tradition acknowledges. Mr. Coomaraswamy opposes the aesthetic approach to the anthropological in favor of the latter; and yet a great deal that is important in Milton Nahm's recent *The Aesthetic Experience and Its Presuppositions* is due to the incorporation of anthropological matter.

Most of all there belongs to aesthetics Kant's hard-won intellectual conquest, the idea of disinterested pleasure or free favor as characteristic of aesthetic contemplation.

When our author says "disinterested aesthetic contemplation is . . . pure non-sense" (*Why Exhibit,* p. 16), he has not taken the trouble to learn what the sentence means. At his best Mr. Coomaraswamy teaches that the right functioning of art is inseparable from a just organization of society and from personal wholeness. It is to be regretted that he often cut himself off—perhaps because of preoccupation with his own languages—from many able allies.

Katharine Everett Gilbert:

A BIBLIOGRAPHY

COMPILED BY LULU C. ERWIN

[*The first three divisions are arranged chronologically; the last, which lists book reviews and notices, is arranged alphabetically by the name of the author whose book is under review.*]

I. BOOKS

Maurice Blondel's Philosophy of Action. ("[University of North Carolina] Studies in Philosophy," No. 1.) Chapel Hill: Department of Philosophy, University of North Carolina, 1924. Pp. v, 94.

Studies in Recent Aesthetics. Chapel Hill: University of North Carolina Press, 1927. Pp. ix, 178.

A History of Esthetics (with Helmut Kuhn). New York: Macmillan, 1939. Pp. xx, 582. A second edition is to be published by the University of Indiana Press in 1952. A Spanish translation was published in 1947 by the Editorial Biblioteca Nueva, Buenos Aires, Argentina.

II. CONTRIBUTIONS TO BOOKS

"Hegel's Criticism of Spinoza," in George Holland Sabine (ed.), *Philosophical Essays in Honor of James Edwin Creighton* (New York: Macmillan, 1917), pp. 26-41.

"Foreword" to Elizabeth Gilmore Holt, *Literary Sources of Art History* (Princeton: Princeton University Press, 1947), pp. vii-viii.

"Historical Survey" under AESTHETICS, in Joseph T. Shipley (ed.), *Dictionary of World Literature* (New York: Philosophical Library, 1947), pp. 8-11.

"The Vital Disequilibrium in Croce's Historicism," in Milton R. Konvitz and Arthur E. Murphy (eds.), *Essays in Political Theory. Presented to George H. Sabine* (Ithaca: Cornell University Press, 1948), pp. 206-27.

"Aesthetics," in *Collier's Encyclopedia* (New York: P. F. Collier & Son, 1949), I, 136-37.

"Cassirer's Placement of Art," in Paul Arthur Schilpp (ed.), *The Philosophy of Ernst Cassirer* (Evanston, Ill.: Library of Living Philosophers, Inc., 1949), pp. 605-30.

III. CONTRIBUTIONS TO PERIODICALS

"The Mind and Its Discipline," *The Philosophical Review*, XXVII (July, 1918), 413-27.

"Philosophical Idealism and Current Practice," *The Philosophical Review*, XXVIII (May, 1919), 301-4.

"Humor and Bosanquet's Theory of Experience," *The Philosophical Review*, XXXI (July, 1922), 352-68.

"The Philosophical Bearings of Biological Psychology," *The Philosophical Review*, XXXII (May, 1923), 294-300.

"The Principle of Reason in the Light of Bosanquet's Philosophy," *The Philosophical Review*, XXXII (Nov., 1923), 599-611.

"The Philosophy of Feeling in Current Poetics," *The Journal of Philosophy*, XX (Nov. 22, 1923), 645-53. A paper read in Dec., 1922, before the American Philosophical Association, Eastern Division, meeting at the Union Theological Seminary.

"Maurice Blondel's Philosophy of Action," *The Philosophical Review*, XXXIII (May, 1924), 273-85. Modified form of the paper read in Dec., 1923, before the American Philosophical Association, Eastern Division, meeting at Brown University.

"James E. Creighton as Writer and Editor," *The Journal of Philosophy*, XXII (May 7, 1925), 256-64. A paper read in Dec., 1924, before the American Philosophical Association, Eastern Division, meeting at Swarthmore College.

"Hardy and the Weak Spectator," *The Reviewer,* V (July, 1925), 9-25.

"The One and the Many in Croce's Aesthetic," *The Philosophical Review,* XXXIV (Sept., 1925), 443-56.

"Hardy's Use of Nature," *The Reviewer,* V (Oct., 1925), 21-33.

"Santayana's Doctrine of Aesthetic Expression," *The Philosophical Review,* XXXV (May, 1926), 221-35.

"What Is Philosophy?," *The South Atlantic Quarterly,* XXVII (Oct., 1928), 355-66. Reprinted in *Fifty Years of The South Atlantic Quarterly* (Durham, N. C.: Duke University Press, 1952), pp. 210-20.

"The Relation of the Moral to the Aesthetic Standard in Plato," *The Philosophical Review,* XLIII (May, 1934), 279-94.

"Aesthetic Imitation and Imitators in Aristotle," *The Philosophical Review,* XLV (Nov., 1936), 558-73.

"The Relation between Esthetics and Art-Criticism," *The Journal of Philosophy,* XXXV (May 26, 1938), 289-95.

"Ruskin's Relation to Aristotle," *The Philosophical Review,* XLIX (Jan., 1940), 52-62.

"Mind and Medium in the Modern Dance," *The Journal of Aesthetics and Art Criticism,* I (Spring, 1941), 106-29.

"Recent Catholic Views on Art and Poetry," *The Journal of Philosophy,* XXXIX (Nov. 19, 1942), 654-61. A paper read in Dec., 1941, before the American Philosophical Association, Eastern Division, meeting at Vassar College.

"The Basis for AAUW Membership," *Journal of American Association of University Women,* XXXVI (Summer, 1943), 254-57.

"The Intent and Tone of Mr. I. A. Richards," *The*

Journal of Aesthetics and Art Criticism, III (April, 1945), 29-48.

"A Spatial Configuration in Five Recent Poets," *The South Atlantic Quarterly,* XLIV (Oct., 1945), 422-31. A paper read Sept. 12, 1944, before the American Society for Aesthetics, meeting at the Cleveland Museum of Art.

"A Reply to Van Meter Ames's 'Note on *A History of Esthetics'*" (with Helmut Kuhn), *The Journal of Aesthetics and Art Criticism,* IV (March, 1946), 187-94.

"Art between the Distinct Idea and the Obscure Soul," *The Journal of Aesthetics and Art Criticism,* VI (Sept., 1947), 21-26.

"Recent Poets on Man and His Place," *The Philosophical Review,* LVI (Sept., 1947), 469-90. Delivered as the presidential address at the meeting of the American Philosophical Association, Eastern Division, at Yale University, Dec. 27, 1946.

"Sguardo all'attività filosofica più recente negli Stati Uniti" (trans. Rina Detti), *Il Ponte* (Florence), IV (June, 1948), 560-66.

Contribution to "Aiken's 'Criteria for an Adequate Aesthetics': A Symposium," *The Journal of Aesthetics and Art Criticism,* VII (Dec., 1948), 148-58.

"Seven Senses of a Room," *The Journal of Aesthetics and Art Criticism,* VIII (Sept., 1949), 1-11. Delivered as the presidential address at the meeting of the American Society for Aesthetics at Harvard University, Sept. 4, 1948.

Guest Editorial: "Architecture and the Poet," *The Journal of the American Institute of Architects,* XIII (March, 1950), 99-102.

"Two Levels of Aesthetic Definition," *The Journal of Aesthetics and Art Criticism,* IX (Dec., 1950), 119-23.

"Poets on the Bridge," *1951 Yearbook of the Poetry Society of Georgia.*

"Clean and Organic: A Study in Architectural Semantics," *The Journal of the Society of Architectural Historians,* X (Oct., 1951), 3-7.

IV. REVIEWS AND NOTICES

Florence Ayscough, *Fir-Flower Tablets*, trans. by Amy Lowell, 1921. *The South Atlantic Quarterly*, XXII (April, 1923), 187-89.

Irving Babbitt, *Rousseau and Romanticism*, 1919. *The Philosophical Review*, XXVIII (Nov., 1919), 629-41.

Albert G. A. Balz, *Idea and Essence in the Philosophies of Hobbes and Spinoza*, 1918. *The Philosophical Review*, XXVII (Nov., 1918), 667-69.

Brand Blanshard, *The Nature of Thought*, 1940. *The South Atlantic Quarterly*, XLI (April, 1942), 224-25.

Franz J. Böhm, *Die Logik der Ästhetik*, 1930. *The Journal of Philosophy*, XXIX (March 3, 1932), 138-39.

Georg Bohrmann, *Spinoza's Stellung zur Religion*, 1914. *The Philosophical Review*, XXIV (Jan., 1915), 111.

Helen Bosanquet, *Bernard Bosanquet. A Short Account of His Life*, 1924. *The South Atlantic Quarterly*, XXIV (Jan., 1925), 101-3.

Emile Boutroux, *The Relation between Thought and Action from the German and from the Classical Point of View*, 1918. *The Philosophical Review*, XXVIII (Jan., 1919), 98-99.

Edwin Berry Burgum (ed.), *The New Criticism: An Anthology of Modern Aesthetics and Literary Criticism*, 1930. *American Literature*, III (March, 1931), 112-14.

R. G. Collingwood, *Outlines of a Philosophy of Art*, 1925. *The South Atlantic Quarterly*, XXV (April, 1926), 200-201.

Ananda K. Coomaraswamy, *Why Exhibit Works of Art?*, 1943; *Figures of Speech or Figures of Thought*, 1946. *The Art Bulletin*, XXX (June, 1948), 157-59.

Benedetto Croce, *An Autobiography*, trans. by R. G. Collingwood, 1927. *The Philosophical Review*, XXXVII (May, 1928), 281-82.

Benedetto Croce, *The Conduct of Life*, 1924. *The Philosophical Review*, XXXVI (May, 1927), 277-79.

Herbert Ernest Cushman, *A Beginner's History of Philosophy*, rev. ed., 1919. *The Philosophical Review*, XXIX (Sept., 1920), 505-6.

John Dewey and Others, *Creative Intelligence. Essays in the Pragmatic Attitude*, 1917. *The Philosophical Review*, XXVIII (March, 1919), 200-208.

Horatio W. Dresser, *A History of Modern Philosophy*, 1928. *The South Atlantic Quarterly*, XXVIII (July, 1929), 330-31.

Curt J. Ducasse, *Art, the Critics, and You*, 1944. *The Philosophical Review*, LIV (Sept., 1945), 612-14.

Curt J. Ducasse, *The Philosophy of Art*, 1929. *American Literature*, II (March, 1930), 99-100.

James H. Dunham, *Freedom and Purpose. An Interpretation of the Psychology of Spinoza*, 1916. *The Philosophical Review*, XXVI (Jan., 1917), 102-4.

G. C. Field, *Moral Theory*, 1921. *The South Atlantic Quarterly*, XXII (July, 1923), 290-93.

Louis W. Flaccus, *The Spirit and Substance of Art*, 3d ed., 1941. *The Journal of Aesthetics and Art Criticism*, II (Fall, 1941), 123.

John Galsworthy, *The White Monkey*, 1924. *The Reviewer*, V (April, 1925), 111-14.

Kate Gordon, *Educational Psychology*, 1917. *The Philosophical Review*, XXVII (May, 1918), 326-27.

Theodore Meyer Greene, *The Arts and the Art of Criticism*, 1940. *The Philosophical Review*, L (Sept., 1941), 535-38.

J. C. Gregory, *The Nature of Laughter*, 1924. *The Journal of Philosophy*, XXI (Dec. 18, 1924), 715-18.

Louis Grudin, *A Primer of Aesthetics: Logical Approaches to a Philosophy of Art*, 1930. *The Philosophical Review*, XLII (Jan., 1933), 74-75.

William A. Hammond, *A Bibliography of Aesthetics and of a Philosophy of the Fine Arts from 1900 to 1932*, rev. ed., 1934. *American Literature*, VI (Jan., 1935), 472-73.

Katharine Everett Gilbert: A Bibliography

Charlotte Hardin, *Coins and Medals*, 1921. *The South Atlantic Quarterly*, XXII (April, 1923), 187-89.

Walter Marshall Horton, *The Philosophy of the Abbé Bautain*, 1926. *The South Atlantic Quarterly*, XXVII (Jan., 1928), 100-102.

John Hospers, *Meaning and Truth in the Arts*, 1946. *The South Atlantic Quarterly*, XLVII (April, 1948), 246-48.

George W. Howgate, *George Santayana*, 1938. *American Literature*, XII (March, 1940), 117-21.

Gabriel Huan, *Le Dieu de Spinoza*, 1914. *The Philosophical Review*, XXIV (Jan., 1915), 110-11.

Lawrence Hyde, *Isis and Osiris*, 1948. *The South Atlantic Quarterly*, XLVIII (April, 1949), 322-23.

C. E. M. Joad, *Common-Sense Ethics*, 1921. *The South Atlantic Quarterly*, XXII (July, 1923), 290-93.

Horace M. Kallen, *Art and Freedom*, Vols. I and II, 1942. *The Philosophical Review*, LIII (March, 1944), 211-15.

Cassius J. Keyser, *Mathematical Philosophy. A Study of Fate and Freedom*, 1922. *The South Atlantic Quarterly*, XXII (April, 1923), 190-91.

Charles Lalo, *Notions d'Esthétique*, 1948. *The Journal of Aesthetics and Art Criticism*, VII (June, 1949), 366-67.

Henry Lanz, *The Physical Basis of Rime. An Essay on the Aesthetics of Sound*, 1931. *The Philosophical Review*, XLII (Nov., 1933), 636-38.

Émile Lasbax, *La Hiérarchie dans l'Univers chez Spinoza*, 1919. *The Philosophical Review*, XXIX (Nov., 1920), 592-93.

K. S. Laurila, *Asthetische Streitfragen*, 1934. *The Philosophical Review*, XLV (March, 1936), 217-18.

Walter Lippman, *A Preface to Morals*, 1929. *The South Atlantic Quarterly*, XXIX (Jan., 1930), 97-98.

Gerhard K. Lomer, *The Concept of Method*, 1910. *The Philosophical Review*, XXII (Sept., 1913), 565-66.

Katharine Everett Gilbert: A Bibliography

Amy Lowell, *Legends*, 1921. *The South Atlantic Quarterly*, XXII (April, 1923), 187-89.

Henry Rutgers Marshall, *The Beautiful*, 1924. *The South Atlantic Quarterly*, XXIV (April, 1925), 213-15.

An Anglo-Saxon Mother, *Hindu Mind Training*, 1917. *The Philosophical Review*, XXVI (Sept., 1917), 564-65.

Joseph Fort Newton, *My Idea of God. A Symposium of Faith*, 1926. *The South Atlantic Quarterly*, XXVI (April, 1927), 206-9.

Helen Huss Parkhurst, *Beauty, an Interpretation of Art and the Imaginative Life*, 1930. *The Philosophical Review*, XLI (Jan., 1932), 82-84.

Johannes Pfeiffer, *Das lyrische Gedicht als ästhetisches Gebilde. Ein phänomenologischer Versuch*, 1931. *The Philosophical Review*, XLV (Jan., 1936), 105.

D. W. Prall, *Aesthetic Judgment*, 1929. *The South Atlantic Quarterly*, XXIX (April, 1930), 212-13.

Frederick Clarke Prescott, *Poetry and Myth*, 1927. *The Philosophical Review*, XXXVII (July, 1928), 385-87.

William Louis Rabenort, *Spinoza as Educator*, 1911. *The Philosophical Review*, XXII (Sept., 1913), 566-67.

Louis Arnaud Reid, *A Study in Aesthetics*, 1931. *The Journal of Philosophy*, XXIX (May 26, 1932), 303-6.

Gustav Theodor Richter, *Spinoza's Philosophische Terminologie*, 1913. *The Philosophical Review*, XXIII (March, 1914), 223-24.

W. H. R. Rivers, *Instinct and the Unconscious: A Contribution to a Biological Theory of the Psychoneuroses*, 1920. *The Philosophical Review*, XXXII (May, 1923), 342-43.

Daniel Sommer Robinson, *An Anthology of Recent Philosophy*, 1929. *The South Atlantic Quarterly*, XXVIII (July, 1929), 330-31.

Richard Rothschild, *Reality and Illusion*, 1934. *The Philosophical Review*, XLV (Jan., 1936), 82-84.

Katharine Everett Gilbert: A Bibliography

Jean-Paul Sartre, *The Psychology of Imagination*, 1948. *The South Atlantic Quarterly*, XLVIII (April, 1949), 303-4.

Paul Arthur Schilpp (ed.), *The Philosophy of George Santayana*, 1940. *American Literature*, XIV (May, 1942), 189.

May Sinclair, *The New Idealism*, 1922. *The Philosophical Review*, XXXII (Jan., 1923), 89-93.

G. Morpurgo Tagliabue, *Il Concetto dello Stile: saggio di una fenomenologia dell'arte*, 1951. To appear in *The Journal of Aesthetics and Art Criticism.*

Miguel de Unamuno, *The Tragic Sense of Life in Men and in Peoples*, 1921. *The Philosophical Review*, XXXII (May, 1923), 340-41.

J. Van Vloten and J. P. N. Land, *Benedicti De Spinoza Opera Quotquot Reperta Sunt*, 1914. *The Philosophical Review*, XXIV (March, 1915), 224-25.

Leone Vivante, *Notes on the Originality of Thought. The Concept of Internal Necessity: Poetic Thought and Constructive Thought*, 1927. *The Journal of Philosophy*, XXV (Sept. 13, 1928), 529-31.

C. N. Wenger, *The Aesthetics of Robert Browning*, 1924. *The Philosophical Review*, XXXV (Jan., 1926), 84-85.

Frederick J. E. Woodbridge, *The Son of Apollo*, 1929. *The South Atlantic Quarterly*, XXIX (Jan., 1930), 111-12.

William Kelley Wright, *A Student's Philosophy of Religion*, 1922. *The Philosophical Review*, XXXI (Nov., 1922), 624-26.